# Turn Every Transaction into an Experience

# TURN EVERY TRANSACTION INTO AN EXPERIENCE

## THE DEFINITIVE GUIDE TO INCREASING CAR BUYERS' LOYALTY

**Douglas Wright**

ISBN-13: 9781546581406
ISBN-10: 1546581405
Library of Congress Control Number: 2017907501
CreateSpace Independent Publishing Platform
North Charleston, South Carolina

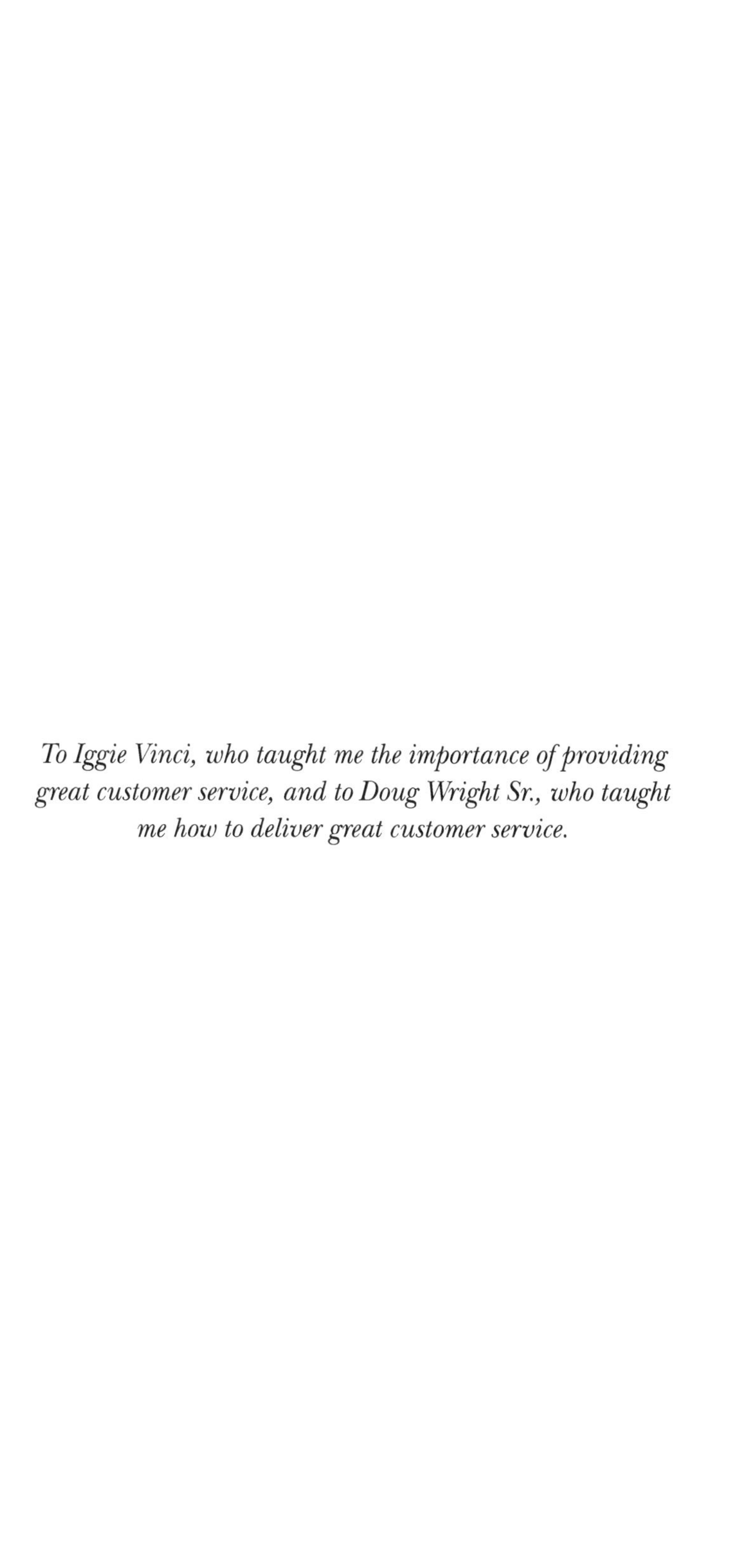

*To Iggie Vinci, who taught me the importance of providing great customer service, and to Doug Wright Sr., who taught me how to deliver great customer service.*

# CONTENTS

# Foreword

Thank you for taking the time to read this book. I want to begin by stating the simple, straightforward goal of this book: to help automotive sales consultants become more successful. I define *success* as selling more vehicles at a higher gross profit while increasing customers' loyalty. Notice that I did not say increasing customers' satisfaction. Many businesses, including the car industry, are fixated on increasing customer satisfaction. First, the term *customer satisfaction* is not what I would strive for. To begin with, I do not think businesses want satisfied customers. If you look up the word *satisfied* in the dictionary, the first synonym that appears is *content.* You should want your customers to be more than just content. The next time your significant other asks you how you feel about your relationship, tell him or her that you are "satisfied"—and then prepare to sleep on the couch. You should want customers who are loyal, not necessarily those who are satisfied. Now, there is somewhat of a correlation between the two qualities, but with loyal customers, you will make more money, and the process will be easier. Loyal customers not only tell others about their experiences at your dealership but also frequently return to your store, so they help lower your advertising and marketing expenses. In addition, loyal customers are easier to sell to because they already like and trust you. If the Sales Process is more enjoyable, fewer sales consultants will leave, thus reducing turnover. Finally, as we all know, loyal customers will spend more on your cars. The reason, as you will see, is that they are not just paying for the cars—they are paying for their experiences, of which you are a big part. The goal of this book is to help YOU sell more cars with a higher gross profit and increased customer loyalty.

I know many dealers and sales consultants who have books on their desks about how other industries (e.g., the hotel and restaurant industries) improve the customer experience. These dealers use these books in an attempt to incorporate what other industries do to be successful. Well, you no longer have to do this. The book you are now reading takes into account not only the best practices from other industries but also the best practices from the automotive industry to show you how to sell cars and increase customer loyalty by turning every transaction into an **experience**.

You will not be learning a new process. You will learn how to EXECUTE your Sales Process in a way that creates loyal customers. Also, to be successful in automotive sales, you must practice the skills outlined in this book and constantly strive to improve. You will need to give a 100 percent effort 100 percent of the time if you want to be successful. This is hard to do. If what we will discuss were easy, everyone would already be doing it. Having said that, keep in mind that this is not rocket science: we are not trying to send a man to Mars; we are selling cars. So while it is hard, it is not difficult. What is more, I will lay it all out for you in a very simple way.

I want to mention one more thing: if you are looking for a book that tells you exactly what to say or do, then you are reading the wrong book. You will learn skills, tools, and techniques—not words to memorize. This book is not designed to tell you exactly what to say verbatim. By reading this book, you will learn how to think differently when it comes to selling cars. I will present scenarios to you, and instead of telling you what to say, I will lay out how you should think to successfully navigate the scenarios. After you change your thought process, you will be more successful than you ever thought possible.

# Introduction

Now that you know my main goal, let me tell you a little about me. I grew up around my father's Mercedes-Benz dealership. Many of the ideas in this book can be traced back to his customer-service philosophy. In addition, I have a master's degree in business administration from Columbia University. After spending a few years on Wall Street, I was drawn back into this business when my brother and I purchased a nonluxury dealership. Unfortunately, I did not use my father's customer-service philosophy when running my own store, and it is probably why I ultimately had to sell that store. However, that experience taught me a great deal. I have spent the last two decades working with several luxury automakers' sales consultants to create a better customer experience. Ultimately, both my automotive experience and my years of research into how successful organizations create great customer experiences have led to this book. As you will see, I use many analogies from outside the car business.

So why did I write this book? Essentially, I am disgusted that well into the twenty-first century, our industry continues to have a poor reputation, and despite numerous "selling systems" being used throughout our industry, grosses are down, dealership loyalty rates are down, and sales volume per sales consultant is stagnant. Now, many of you may be thinking that I am only creating hyperboles for the sake of selling this book. Well, let us look at some third-party statistics. According to an Autotrader study that took place in 2015, only 17 percent of customers like the car-buying process—only 17 percent! If you somehow think we have improved over the last thirty years, think again. Edmunds.com found that nine out of ten customers wished that shopping for cars were easier. Customers are buying cars that, in many cases, require the equivalent of half a year's salary, and they dread entering dealerships to buy those cars.

Make no mistake: we have created this problem. What other industry uses phrases like *steal their trade* or *lay down* to describe customers? If you want to steal something from your customers, do not expect them to be loyal customers. *Lay down* is an interesting term. It refers to customers who are easy to sell to and spend at or near list prices. I would think that these people should be considered your best customers. Instead of referring to them in a positive manner, we use a derogatory term like *lay down* and then wonder why our customers do not like to come into our dealerships. I know what you are thinking: our customers do not hear us say such words. However, the words you use in your dealership will spawn a culture that has historically treated customers poorly. It is not 1975 or even 2005. The historical way of selling cars will not work today, and I hope that the old way soon becomes extinct in today's world.

The historical way of selling cars was not transparent. Customers were provided information on a need-to-know basis. Sales consultants would cover up half of the paper and say, "Just sign here." Sales consultants are still being told to *control* their customers. This term has been interpreted to mean that customers should be "pulled" or "grabbed" and dragged through the Sales Process—that is, in a metaphorical sense. When the concept of control is combined with a lack of transparency, we get sales processes that are manipulative and use tricks to get customers to do what the sales consultants want them to do. Such sales processes have led to vehicle sales consultants being ranked last in a Gallup survey that asked customers to rate the honesty and ethical standards of people in different professions. Sales consultants have stopped throwing customers' keys on the roof to prevent them from leaving, but they still manipulate the customers by saying things like "follow me" as they walk out of the dealership and toward the demonstration vehicles. It should come as no surprise that loyalty rates at most dealerships hover in the 23 percent range and that brand loyalty is over 50 percent. That means that there is a 50 percent chance that when one of your customers returns to the market, he or she will buy the same brand of vehicle that you sold that person during your previous encounter. However, the odds are that such customers will buy those same vehicles from other dealerships. That needs to stop. This book will show you how you can retain customers.

If only 17 percent of customers like the car-buying process, then why do you think they would go to a car dealership? That is right: they have to buy cars. If you do not like to do something, then the only reason you would do it is if you had to. This explains why McKinsey & Company found that the average customer visits fewer than two dealerships. Of course this makes sense: since people hate the car-buying experience, why would they want to visit more? However, people's dislike for car dealerships does not mean—despite what you might have heard—that people want to buy cars online.

## Online Car Buying

According to the media, consumers do not want to talk to sales consultants, they do not want to negotiate, and they want to be able to buy cars online and have them delivered to their homes. I understand, as I stated earlier, that customers do not like the car-buying process. However, that does not mean that they want to do everything online. Keep in mind that if a person does not trust a process, then the last thing he or she will want to do is move that process online, where there are no face-to-face interactions. According to Jason Dorsey, founder of the Center for Generational Kinetics, even millennials (whom we will discuss in more detail later) "still find comfort and confidence in having contact with a human being when it comes to financing a major purchase, like a vehicle." His point is an important one, not only because it relates to millennials. Consumers may purchase clothing, food, and even electronics online, but for the second-largest purchase (in some cases, the largest purchase they will ever make), they want to do it face-to-face.

According to DealerSocket's 2016 Dealership Action Report, only 33 percent of consumers would like to be able to buy a car online without visiting a dealership. In Autotrader's Car Buyer of the Future study, 84 percent of consumers indicated that they want to buy a car in person. In addition, 43 percent of consumers see dealerships as places to learn from. Also, 56 percent of consumers, including over 50 percent of women and millennials, prefer to negotiate over flat-rate pricing. According to Autotrader, this last percentage is a result of the fact that consumers do not trust flat-rate pricing and that they feel they have to negotiate to get fair prices. Finally, while price is important to consumers, it is not the be-all and end-all that the media and consultants would have you believe. According to the Autotrader study, 54 percent of consumers are willing to buy from dealerships that offer the consumers' preferred experiences—*even if the dealerships do not have the lowest prices*—and 73 percent of consumers will drive farther just to reach great sales consultants. According to DealerRater, customers who are happy with their vehicle purchases are more likely to recommend the sales consultants than the stores. Of consumers surveyed, 70 percent said they would recommend their sales consultants, while only 30 percent would recommend the dealerships they went to. My goal is to make YOU one of those valued sales consultants. According to a DrivingSales.com study, auto sales could rise about 25 percent if the retail experience improved. Just think about that for a moment. You could sell 25 percent more cars just by having a better process. Hopefully, you are beginning to understand why I wrote this book.

Despite car buyers' dislike for the car-buying process, they still want to visit dealerships and buy vehicles from sales consultants willing to negotiate. Consumers just want the process to be better. In fact, an Autotrader survey revealed that 72 percent of consumers would visit dealerships more often if the buying process was improved. In this book, we will concentrate on elevating the customer experience, which will lead to increases in cars sold, gross profits, and loyalty. The approach described in this book is not a selling system. Systems are used to sell timeshares, not to create great customer experiences. The execution of the Sales Process described in this book will allow you to guide your customers through the process rather than pull them through.

## Not Just the Steak

I mentioned that I would use analogies from outside the car business, so here is one such analogy. Imagine that you are at a Ruth's Chris Steak House. You have just enjoyed a ten-ounce filet mignon that is forty-five dollars, which was recommended by your waiter, based on your tastes. Another waiter has replenished your drink without you noticing it. A napkin on your lap matches the color of your pants. A valet is about to bring around your car. After two hours, you are on your way home, thinking about the great food and personalized service you received. Now, imagine you are at Applebee's, and the waiter brings you the *exact* same steak you had at Ruth's Chris Steak House. However, nothing else about the experience is the same. Everything else that happens is typical of Applebee's: your plate is not hot, the waiter suggests the same dish to everyone at the table, the drinks take forever to arrive, and you use several paper napkins. Finally, after forty-five minutes of dining, you receive the check and see that Applebee's is charging you forty-five dollars for the steak. How do you feel?

Both restaurants have the same process for delivering your dinner. However, the execution of the process is much different at both restaurants. First, you would be willing to spend two hours dining at a Ruth's Chris Steak House but would never spend two hours at an Applebee's. In addition, you would be annoyed if the Ruth's Chris Steak House rushed you out after forty-five minutes. Finally, you would not be willing to pay forty-five dollars for the same exact steak at Applebee's, even though it would be the same as the one you had at the Ruth's Chris Steak House. Why? Because the Applebee's would not execute its process like the steak house.

What does all of this have to do with selling cars? If sales consultants try to sell vehicles with a process similar to Applebee's, customers are not going to spend MSRP for new vehicles.

Many car sales consultants are concentrating on using an Applebee's like process, and they even try to decrease the time customers spend at their dealerships. The thinking is that customers do not want to spend hours buying a car, so sales consultants need to reduce the time customers spend at dealerships. This way of thinking looks at the problem too simplistically. If consumers do not like the ways certain products are sold, then they will always answer surveys by stating that they would be happier with different sales processes. Consumers will also suggest that the relevant processes should be quicker.

Car buyers are purchasing a product that is the equivalent of half of their yearly salary. Think about that. These same customers go to a mall and spend hours shopping for products that are less than a day's salary, yet we think the car-buying process needs to be quicker? Customers like the shopping experience at the mall, so they are willing to invest their time. Car buyers are about to buy the second largest purchase of their lives, so they should be excited. When people buy the largest purchase of their lives (i.e., a house) and when they make smaller purchases (e.g., a new cell phone), they get excited. On the other hand, car buyers are not excited about purchasing cars because they hate the way the Sales Process is executed. "Making the bad process go faster does not make it better." If my dentist decreased the time I was there by half, I would still not enjoy the visit. Why not make the execution of the process better? For example, the Sales Process could be executed in a way that would not waste customers' time. Too many dealers are concentrating on one part of a nine-step Sales Process. To truly exceed customers' expectations and to make the car-buying process exciting again, sales consultants need to execute the entire process (not just one or two steps) in a customer-focused way.

Cars are becoming more expensive and complicated, especially with the advent of more and more autonomous driving features. This requires customers to buy vehicles from dealerships in person. Customers think the process is too long and want it to be shorter or different because they do not like the current way of selling cars. Stop thinking about how to make the Sales Process quicker; instead, start thinking about how to make it "better." By the way, executing the Sales Process in a better and more efficient way will inevitably take less time. However, the time will be less not because you concentrated on making the Sales Process quicker but because you concentrated on making it better. This book will guide you on how to execute the automotive Sales Process in a better way.

The better way of selling cars focuses on elevating the customer experience. Elevating the customer experience is about much more than having loaner cars, washing cars when they are in for service, and having a cappuccino bar. It is about executing a process that elevates the customer experience. The businesses that elevate the customer experience are all businesses that execute their processes in a customer-focused way.

The success of Starbucks is not only due to the fact that they serve a quality cup of coffee but also due to how they execute the process of delivering that cup of coffee. For example, by writing customers' names on their cups, the baristas personalize the experience. Instead of having to shout, "Grande caramel macchiato," a barista will say, "John, your drink is ready." This is a small part of the execution of the coffee company's process, yet it elevates the customer experience.

I travel a great deal, so I always order room service, and I always order dessert. Typically, my dessert involves a piece of cake or pie à la mode. Usually, one of the hotel staff will bring me my dinner, but by the time I get to my dessert, the ice cream will have melted. At the Vancouver Marriott, the hotel staff executes this process differently. They will deliver my room-service order but without the dessert. When I once asked about the dessert, they stated that they would bring it up in fifteen minutes so that the ice cream would not be melted. They elevated my experience by executing their room-service process better. Elevating the customer experience is about executing the Sales Process better than everyone else.

## Women and Car Buying

Finally, it is amazing to me that in the twenty-first century, we still need to discuss the topic of how to sell to women, yet here we are. Despite years of everyone telling dealers and sales consultants that women should be taken seriously when they visit dealerships, some dealerships (along with the manufacturers in some cases) often treat those women as second-class citizens. Advertising, marketing, and even brochures tend to be geared toward men. Sales consultants who speak only to a man when he is accompanied by a woman or who try to sell a woman a car by appealing to how she will look in the vehicle are reinforcing the stereotype that dealerships are old boys' clubs. This stereotype is reinforced further by the lack of female employees and by a culture that uses such terms as *roach, the box, stroke, drop pants,* and *lay down* to describe customers, their actions, or their trade-ins. Obviously, using such terms needs to end.

The economic impact of the old boys' club behavior is significant. First, here are some statistics. Women purchase 54 percent of all cars in the United States and influence 85 percent of all car-buying decisions. Women do not just influence their spouses; through social media, women are influencing friends and relatives as well. In addition, four out of ten women earn more than their husbands. Because the majority of college degrees are now being awarded to women, this trend will continue. I want you to reread this paragraph. The next time you see a woman enter your dealership, remember 85 percent. So how do you sell to women in a way that will have them buy from you and tell their friends about you? By turning every transaction into an **experience**.

# CHAPTER 1

## MILLENNIALS

Millennials are one of today's hot topics. Everyone is talking about how to capture this younger generation. I want to dispel some common misconceptions regarding millennials. However, before we reveal the misconceptions about millennials, let us define the generation. Even the definition of millennials is misunderstood. News media and automotive consultants define millennials differently to make their points. If the data do not support what they are saying, they just change the definition of what a millennial is. That is why you often hear different dates associated with the term. For our purposes, I will use the definition from the US Census Bureau since it collects demographic information. According to the agency, millennials are people born between 1982 and 2000. The agency states that millennials number 83.1 million people. Also, according to the agency, baby boomers are those people born within the years 1946–1964, and they number 75.4 million people. Generation X is between baby boomers and millennials (1965–1981) and number 65 million people. Now, the two big misconceptions about millennials are the following: First, they do not buy cars. Second (and here is the oxymoron), in order to be successful, car dealers need to understand how to sell to this generation. So let me get this straight. They are not buying cars, but car dealers need to change their Sales Processes to accommodate them. Crazy.

For years, we have been made to believe that millennials (regardless of how we define them) do not want to buy cars. We have been told that this generation of young people does not need or want cars. They can connect with their friends through social media, Skype, and FaceTime; thus, the freedom and connection that the Internet provides mean that millennials do not need cars. In addition, when they want to go places, they often use Uber or other car-sharing services. Well, lo and behold, millennials actually do want to buy cars. As reported by Bloomberg's David Welch, "Millennials...are more captivated by cars than their parents and still want the freedom of owning one, according to a new study from the San Diego consulting firm Strategic Vision, Inc. This contradicts predictions in recent years that auto sales would suffer as millennials, also known as generation Y, took Uber instead of buying their own vehicles." This comment was reinforced by the Associated Press's article "4 Reasons Millennials Are Buying Cars in Big Numbers." So why was everyone wrong? I believe a big reason was that people wanted to believe what they wanted to believe.

In the twenty-first century, new technologies and new ways of doing things are constantly being created. The Internet, cell phones, apps, car sharing, Uber, hybrid vehicles, and so forth, are exciting and new. We all want to believe that this younger generation will be different, will use these new technologies, and will abandon the old ways of doing things. With this mind-set, we may easily slip into thinking that young people are so environmentally conscious and tech savvy that they could not possibly want cars. However, from my experience with my children, I learned that young people want cars. Not everyone lives in New York City. Most of us live in suburbs, where young people want and need cars.

There is more to the story, though. It is true that young people are buying cars later in their lives. The reason has more to do with circumstances than with desires. First, the advent of graduated licensing laws, which make teens practice driving in stages before they receive full licenses, is one reason why in 2010 only 69 percent of nineteen-year-olds had driver's licenses versus 87 percent in 1983. Second, the Great Recession hit this demographic very hard, and millennial unemployment reached upward of 13 percent, which delayed millennials' car buying. Finally, this is a generation in which the people, for numerous reasons, have put off everything in their lives, such as getting married, having children, and leaving home. Buying a car is just one more activity that this generation has delayed, in comparison with previous generations. What does all of this mean to you? Instead of paying attention to the names of generations, concentrate on the numbers.

I would like to provide some statistics that were published by the US Census Bureau and the Federal Reserve. I will do my best to make these numbers as easy to understand as possible. First, according to the Federal Reserve's 2015 article "The Young and the Carless? The Demographics of New Vehicle Purchases," people in the age group 16–34 were responsible for 22.6 percent of the new-vehicle purchases. This number is down from 28.6 percent in 2000. Given what was revealed earlier about this younger generation putting off car buying, this makes sense. In addition, people over fifty-five years old were responsible for 36.4 percent of new-vehicle purchases in 2015. In 2000, this same group was responsible for only 21.2 percent of new-vehicle purchases. This trend is being driven by the increase in the age of the US population. For example, in 2000 there were 79 million people in the age group 15–34, which represented 28 percent of the population. In 2015, there were 88 million people in the age group 15–34, which still represented 28 percent of the population.

Now, compare this with people in the age group 55–74. In 2000, there were 42 million people in the age group 55–74, which represented 15 percent of the population. In 2015, there were 68 million people in the age group 55–74, which represented 21 percent of the population. The age group over fifty-five is increasing at a much faster rate than the 15–34 age group. This will continue until 2030. Based on the US Census Bureau's projections for 2030, the people in the age group 15–34 will number 90 million, or 25 percent of the population, and there will be 78 million people in the age group 55–74, which will represent 22 percent of the population. To illustrate, take a look at the following table:

| | AGE 15 - 34 | | | | AGE 55 - 74 | | |
|---|---|---|---|---|---|---|---|
| YEAR | Number (in millions) | % of Population | % Vehicles Purchased | | Number (in millions) | % of Population | % Vehicles Purchased |
| 2000 | 79 | 28% | 28.6% | | 42 | 15% | 21.2% |
| 2015 | 88 | 28% | 22.6% | | 68 | 21% | 36.4% |
| 2020 | 89 | 27% | | | 76 | 23% | |
| 2025 | 90 | 26% | | | 78 | 23% | |
| 2030 | 90 | 25% | | | 78 | 22% | |

*Data for years 2020 - 2030 are projections from US Census bureau*

If these trends continue (it is hard to argue that they will not), it is unlikely that in 2020 the news media's projection that 40 percent of the new-car purchases will be made by millennials will be accurate, regardless of which years we use to define them. You can interpret this data differently, but the way that I interpret it is that people over fifty-five will represent the largest market of car buyers in the immediate future.

Now, even if a portion of the vehicles purchased by people over fifty-five are for their younger children, that does not change the fact that you should be concentrating on how to sell to the fifty-five-plus age group more so than on how to sell to millennials. First, unlike other generations, millennials value their parents' opinions. This generation's dads were not the CEOs of the families, nor were the moms the COOs. Millennials grew up in families in which everything revolved around the children. Previous generations of children were told that they should be seen and not heard. As for millennials, they are their parents' friends. In addition, many millennials live at home longer, which also contributes to relationships in which they strongly value their parents' opinions. So even if millennials are solely responsible for purchasing their vehicles, their parents (who are likely over the age of fifty-five) play major roles in those purchases. Moreover, millennials are putting off things until later in life, but people over fifty-five are doing the same.

People are now retiring later in life. This is partly due to the fact that they still have millennials at home to support; also, people are living longer and therefore working longer. This means that people over fifty-five will purchase more vehicles in their remaining lives than other generations. The RV industry is going through a tremendous growth spurt because the industry expects, based on the demographics, that their year-over-year sales will continue to increase for at least the next eleven years. In addition, why do you think that cars have become less popular and that crossovers and SUVs are becoming more popular? Being someone over fifty, I can tell you that it is much easier on the knees, back, and so forth, to get in and out of a crossover or SUV rather than a car. So stop obsessing about millennials, and just sell cars. If you sell them by turning every transaction into an **experience**, you will attract all of the main age groups.

# CHAPTER 2

## TRANSACTION VERSUS EXPERIENCE

At this point, you may be wondering how does our elevating the customer experience relate to the title of this book, which is *Turn Every Transaction into an* ***Experience.*** Let us start by defining the word *experience* and contrast it with the word *transaction.* According to *Merriam-Webster,* a *transaction* is "an exchange or transfer of goods, services, or funds, an action or activity involving two parties that reciprocally affect or influence each other." On the other hand, an *experience* is "a direct observation of or participation in events, something personally encountered, undergone, or lived through, the act or process of directly perceiving events." Perhaps the best way to think about these words is that a transaction is a simple exchange of money for something. For instance, a customer may give you money or a check for a car. An experience is something you remember. Here are some examples of transactions and experiences:

- Picking up a marriage license at a city hall is a transaction. A wedding is an experience.
- The date of your birthday is a transaction. A surprise birthday party is an experience.

- Being greeted by a restaurant's host who says, "Welcome to ABC," is a transaction. Being greeted by a restaurant's host who says, "Welcome, Mr. and Mrs. Smith. Happy twentieth anniversary," is an experience.

To quote Danny Meyer, the owner of Union Square Hospitality Group, "The companies that are going to prevail realize it's the quality of the emotional experience that sets them apart. Service is how well something is done technically; hospitality is how it feels emotionally." People remember and want to share experiences, not transactions. Before we discuss how to create these great experiences, I want to share some examples from other industries.

The most successful companies in almost every customer-facing industry are the ones that concentrate on creating positive experiences for their customers. Many of these businesses are in industries that, like the car business, have low margins, yet they create great experiences for their customers—experiences that keep their customers loyal. As mentioned earlier, one of the ways Starbucks creates a great experience and personalizes it is by asking for customers' names.

The grocery-store industry arguably has the lowest margins. Typical grocery stores compete on prices. I am sure that you have seen the weekly circular in your Sunday newspaper with your local grocery store's coupons. By competing on prices, grocery stores are concentrating on the transactional aspects of their business. Many of them also feature self-checkouts, which allow customers to get through the process more quickly. Like the prices, the speed of a process is a transactional aspect. Grocery stores that focus on transactional aspects will not create loyalty. For example, no one will remain loyal to a grocery store just because it has self-checkout stations. Moreover, certain grocery stores might have the lowest prices for certain items, but as soon as competing grocery stores lower their prices, the customers will switch. If grocery stores continue to lower their prices, they will go out of business ultimately. Contrast such grocery stores with the ones that focus on creating positive experiences for their customers.

Uncle Giuseppe's, an Italian-themed grocery store, recently opened near my home. The owner of this grocery store (who also owns five others in the area) said he wanted to "create stores that mix grocery shopping with a trip down memory lane." His stores are designed to "re-create the way our grandparents used to shop. We want to give people the experience of going to buy meat and having the butcher know their names." To achieve this, the owner designed the layout of the store to look like "the old neighborhood," in which the employees have to get to know their customers and especially their names. What is more, the owner's grocery stores each have a roving singer serenading the shoppers with Frank Sinatra songs. Perhaps the best grocery store chain in the country, Wegmans, is all about the customer experience.

Wegmans does not offer home deliveries because it wants its customers to experience its way of doing business. Not only does Wegmans consistently rank as one of the top grocery stores in the country, based on customer service, but also it does everything it can to make sure that its customers never consider shopping at other grocery stores. For example, Wegmans recently introduced its own app, which allows customers to make a shopping list. However, the app also allows other family members to access the list, so everyone can add his or her own items to it. Moreover, customers can scan the bar codes of items in their homes, such as a milk carton about to be thrown away, and those items will be added to customers' shopping lists. Finally, when customers enter the company's stores, the app will arrange their lists based on the aisle configuration of the Wegmans they are at. Wegmans has such high loyalty rates because it focuses on creating a better experience rather than on offering lower prices.

Even fast-food restaurants are starting to realize that they cannot compete on the transactional aspects of their business. The fast-food chain Taco Bell is rolling out a slightly more upscale version of itself, called the Cantina, and it will have an open kitchen where diners can see their food being prepared. In a pitch to retail landlords, the company said, "We are changing from food as fuel to food as an experience."

Coffee shops, grocery stores, and fast-food restaurants are increasing customer loyalty by turning every transaction into an **experience**. These businesses are in industries that have low margins and are not usually referenced when someone talks about great customer experiences. Sound familiar? Let me show you how you and your dealership can exist in an industry with historically low margins and poor customer service while making high grosses and creating loyal customers by turning every transaction into an **experience**.

# CHAPTER 3

## BUILDING VALUE

Build value! As a sales consultant, you have been told to do this thousands of times. Your manager is constantly telling you to not drop the price but to build value. You have read in sales books about the virtue of building value. I will now tell you something you probably did not know: you can build value by reducing prices. This is not what you want to do, but it can be done. Before I explain, let me first state what should be the main goal of you and everyone at your dealership.

Every process and the execution of every process at your dealership should be implemented with one goal in mind: *increase the likelihood of the customer doing business with you today and in the future.* This is the goal of every touch point, starting with the Greeting (which involves everyone who greets customers, such as receptionists, porters, and cashiers) and going through the Sales Process to the Delivery and Follow-Up. This means that you need to examine not only each step in the Sales Process but also the transitions between steps and everything in each step. In other words, to ensure that the execution of the entire Sales Process is achieving this goal, you may very well need to examine what other nonsales consultants are doing and saying to your customers. This goal comes from the equation that guides *all* purchasing behavior—not just car buying. Every customer purchases or does not purchase a product or service based on the following equation:

Value = Benefit – Cost

Value is that which determines if a purchase is worth buying. For example, if you go into an electronics store to buy a TV and the price is $800, you may decide to not buy it because the price makes it not worth buying. However, a sales consultant ends up offering you a $300 coupon, so you decide that buying the TV at the new cost, $500, is worth it. You end up purchasing the TV—but it did not change! The Value of the TV went up because the price, or cost, went down.

Here is the example in the equation format. You decide that the Benefit of this particular TV is seven hundred. Therefore, the Value of the TV is negative (i.e., 700 – 800 = –100). However, when the price drops to $500, the Value increases to two hundred (700 – 500 = 200). In other words, the higher the Value, the more likely a customer will buy what is being sold. This should not be a surprise since we all want things that are VALUABLE, and by definition, Valuable means that a product or service has a high Value. So if you want to have a customer buy what you are selling, you just need to increase the Value. This brings us back to our equation:

Value = Benefit – Cost

Cost is the price—the transactional aspects. Benefit is what a customer personally receives as a result of doing business with you. These are the **experiential** aspects.

Value is the likelihood of customers' doing business with you. The higher the Value, the more likely customers will do business with you, which is why your goal is to increase the likelihood of the customers' doing business with you today and in the future.

Since you can build value by reducing cost, you need to start stating "build benefits" rather than "build value." In addition, you need to look at not just the benefits of the product or service, but also at how the product or service is delivered, and at all the ancillary items as well (location, treatment, amenities, vocabulary used, dress, etc.). For example, if a waiter at a Ruth's Chris Steak House was wearing sweatpants and delivered your steak on a paper plate with a paper napkin and if your drink was served in a paper cup, you would not spend forty-five dollars for the steak, even though the steak did not change. Therefore, you need to examine everything that goes into the execution of your Sales Process to ensure that it builds benefits.

Customers' purchase decisions are based on Value, even though they may not refer to it as that. They determine what the products' or services' benefits are to them and then attach costs or prices that will make the purchases worthwhile or have a relatively high Value. Customers looking to purchase vehicles do some relevant research, so when they come into dealerships, they have general ideas of the benefits of their desired vehicles. They also know that to gain positive Value they need to get the price or cost to match the Benefit. However, since the Value will be zero or slightly positive, customers will always have buyer's remorse, thinking that they could have increased the Value even more by lowering the price.

Keep in mind that if sales consultants just discuss price they can actually reduce the Value of the vehicle to their customer. Let me explain this further. For example, a customer—after doing his or her own research—determines the Benefit of a particular vehicle. Let us say the customer places the Benefit of a $25,000 car at $23,000. Now, the customer does not want to buy the car for $23,000 because the Value would only be zero (23,000 – 23,000 = 0), so it would not be valuable enough. So the customer tries to buy it for $21,000, which would make the Value $2,000 (23,000 – 21,000 = 2,000). When the customer visits a dealership, a sales consultant informs the customer that his or her price will not work for the relevant vehicle and begins to negotiate with the customer. After negotiating, they arrive at the selling price, or cost, of $22,500. Because the customer was all about the price, the sales consultant never took the opportunity to build the Benefit—he or she just dealt with the price. Because the sale price is $22,500 and because the Benefit does not change from $23,000, the customer's Value goes down from $2,000 to $500 (23,000 – 22,500). The sales consultant makes more on the transaction than what the customer is hoping for, but because the sales consultant did not build up the Benefit, the customer sees the Value of this car go from $2,000 to $500. This kind of drop will create buyer's remorse. By the way, let's look at the following scenarios:

If the sales consultant sold the car for the same price but increased the Benefit by doing everything we will be discussing in this book, then this would happen:

a. Benefit ($25,000) – Cost ($22,500) = $2,500 Value, which would be greater than what the customer originally determined through his or her own research.
b. In the first scenario, the customer would question the fairness of the price paid. In this scenario, the customer would pay the same amount but would believe that he or she did get a fair price.

As you will see in the pages that follow, you should want not only to increase the benefits of the vehicles but also to convey the benefits of you and your dealership through the execution of the Sales Process. By elevating the customer experience, you will increase the Benefit of the customer doing business with you and your dealership. In addition, if you truly sell cars by elevating the customer experience, then over time *you* will become the Benefit to the customer. Sales consultants sometimes change the brand of cars they sell and get their customers to change as well, and they manage to do so because they become the Benefit to their customers—so much so that the Benefit of the sales consultants outweigh the brand of the vehicles!

Before we leave this chapter, we need to discuss two words we often hear when discussing benefits: *feature* and *function.* A feature is what something is, and a function is what that something can do. Once again, a benefit is what a customer receives as a result of a feature. For example, heated seats are a feature. The function is that the seats warm up to different temperatures, depending on the setting. The benefit is that when customers get into their cars after doing something that made them very cold, such as spending an afternoon ice skating, the heated seats will warm their backsides up. The key with features, functions, and benefits is that the features and functions never change. The benefits change depending on the guests. In the example I just gave, the benefit I mentioned would only work with customers who like to ice-skate. If customers do not ice-skate, I would have to find another way to describe the benefit. As long as the benefits are positive, the Value will increase. Notice that the words *feature* and *function* do not appear in the Value Equation. You can tell your customers about all of the features in your vehicles and never actually increase Value. Only after you get to know your customers well enough can you take features and their functions and connect them to things you know about the customers to show them the benefits of the particular features. In this way, you will personalize the experience for the customers.

# CHAPTER 4

## TRUST

You probably did not think you would see a chapter titled "Trust" in a book about selling cars. Yet to truly elevate customers' experience, you must build their trust in you, in your dealership, and in your vehicles. Establishing trust begins with the proper execution of the Sales Process. When customers pull into your lot, their trust in you starts very low. I am sure that the following will not surprise you: according to a recent study, "only 21 percent of people claim that car sales consultants are trustworthy." This belief is one more piece of the baggage that those of us in the car business carry because of the historical way cars were sold.

A major reason why people do not trust car sales consultants is the fact that historically the Sales Process was executed in a nontransparent way. Perhaps you do not cover half the paper and simply ask for customers' signatures anymore, but telling a customer to "follow me" is not transparent. If you want to increase trust, you need to execute the Sales Process in a transparent way.

When customers enter dealerships, their trust is low and their anxiety is high. We all become anxious when we do not know what is going to happen next, or sometimes previous bad experiences overshadow what we are about to do. You must remember that your customers can become anxious quite easily and that everything you do when you are with them will either increase their trepidation or increase their trust in you. When anxiety is high, trust is low; when trust is high, anxiety is low. If you build trust, you will increase the likelihood that your customers do business with you—which is the goal. You can increase trust by enhancing your customers' experience. Cultivating trust happens when you are transparent in the execution of your Sales Process.

To be transparent, you must do the following when you engage your customers: tell them what is going to happen next, tell them the benefits of the next step, and then ask for permission to proceed.

## What Is Going to Happen Next?

Historically, when sales consultants wanted customers to do certain things, they would try to manipulate the customers. As we already discussed, our telling customers to follow us will not increase their trust. If we want to be truly transparent, we need to tell our customers what will happen next. It is such a basic concept, yet sales consultants for years have been devising other words to use rather than just telling their customers what they would like them to do. If you want a customer to go on a demonstration drive, you need to say something similar to "Mr. Smith, I would like to take you on a demonstration drive." I know what you are thinking: "If I told my customers that, then they would say no." Of course they would, because you only did one part of the process.

## The Benefit to Them of the Next Step

When you want your customers to do certain things but you do not want to manipulate them, then you must tell them the benefits of the next step. If I were to tell you the benefits of doing something and then asked you if you wanted to do it, you would answer yes. Well, when you want your customers to do certain things, then you need to describe how they would benefit. If the reasons are true benefits, then their answers will always be yes. Now, you might think that this is also manipulative. Well, you are right. However, the difference is related to the different definitions of manipulation. The first definition of *manipulate* is "to manage dishonestly." The historical way of selling cars, by saying things like "follow me," embraces that definition. I prefer the second definition of the word, which is "to handle skillfully." For example, let us say you are dealing with a male customer, and you want to get him to go on a demonstration drive. Instead of just telling him to follow you, say something like the following: "Mr. Smith, I would like to take you on a demonstration drive to show you the comfortable seating and lumbar support because you mentioned to me that you have a bad back." In this example, I gave the customer a reason why the demonstration drive would benefit him. Now, how did I know about the bad back? Well, I listened during the Needs Assessment Step. Nothing happens in a vacuum. If I had not done a proper analysis of the customer's needs, then I would have to fall back on telling him to follow me to the demonstration drive, yet my doing so would not increase his trust. Telling customers the reasons why the next steps would benefit them will get them to say yes more often and will build their trust in you. In addition, you can enhance the customer experience by personalizing the benefits. In the example, the benefits relieved the male customers' bad back.

## Ask for Permission to Proceed

Finally, the best way to increase trust is to ask customers for permission to move to the next step. When customers have the option of saying yes or no, they feel as though they are in control, which helps to cultivate trust. However, keep in mind that customers may feel that they can say no, but because of the way you asked the question—by stating the relevant benefits—the answers the customers give will always be yes. We will uncover opportunities to use the concept of building trust as we go through each step in the Sales Process.

# CHAPTER 5

## Communication Skills

Communication skills are what ultimately separate good sales consultants from great sales consultants. Fortunately for you, I am going to provide you with the skills and tools to be a great automotive sales consultant. In the next few chapters, you will discover the difference between listening and hearing and the different ways we communicate. You will also learn how you can use these skills to be better at selling, and you will learn the most important skill you need: the ability to ask good questions, which is paramount to life as a whole, not just to selling cars.

Since communication skills are such an important component of elevating the customer experience, we will start by describing how people generally communicate. People communicate with others through the use of words, tone, and body language. Studies have consistently shown that the main way we communicate is through our body language (55 percent), our tone (38 percent), and finally our words (7 percent). These percentages are not surprising because we have all heard the expression "It's not what you say but how you say it." Yet in the car business, we spend an inordinate amount of time concentrating on our words rather than on our body language or tone. You have probably heard a manager say, "Here is what I want you to say to customers." I have yet to hear a manager say, "Here is *how* I would like you to say it."

As we examine each of the ways people communicate, you will find that the ways are all related. What I mean is that smiling (body language) will affect your tone, and that is why employees are told to smile when they speak with customers on the telephone, even though the customers cannot see the employees. Moreover, choosing certain words can also help you convey the correct tone as well. Outside of your tone of voice, though, words and body language stand on their own. Let us begin by discussing the most important communication method—body language.

## Body Language

The Internet contains a tremendous amount of information on body language. The following are some common body-language techniques, you need to stay away from:

- Crossing your arms, which can convey defensiveness
- Not looking a person in the eyes intermittently, which can convey that you cannot be trusted
- Fidgeting, which also can convey untrustworthiness
- Standing with your hands in your pocket, which can convey unprofessionalism

These are some common body-language techniques that you need to use:

- Smiling will make your tone sound better, and people will like you.
- Using your hands confidently to make your points will convey confidence in what you are saying.

- Keeping your head up and your hands at your side or clasped in front of you or behind your back will convey confidence.
- Using intermittent eye contact will help to build trust. When your customers are talking, you will most likely look at their mouths (something we all naturally do); however, when you start speaking, you need to look them in their eyes. If you do not, your customers will not trust you. They will believe that you are hiding something from them. By switching between looking at their mouths to looking at their eyes, you will convey that you are looking at them without staring.

Always pay attention to two things: be aware of what your body language conveys, and always read your customers' body language. In some situations, customers may say all the correct things, but if their body language conveys something else, focus on interpreting their body language to guide you in what you should discuss next with these customers. To fully comprehend and master what your body language conveys, you need to record yourself, or you can have someone watch you with customers and give you feedback.

## Tone

The tone of voice you use with a customer will depend on where you are in the Sales Process. During the Greeting and Needs Assessment, you should convey a conversational tone; during the Presentation, you should convey an enthusiastic tone. However, keep in mind that being aware of your tone and using the correct tone in the correct stages of the process are challenging to master. If you are in a bad mood or thinking about something else, your tone will be affected. In addition, the words you choose can affect your tone. If you use only a few words to ask a plethora of questions, rifling one off after another, you may come across as having a very gruff tone. For example, if you ask a customer what he or she will use a particular car for, who will be the primary driver, and how many miles he or she usually drives—all without letting the customer catch his or her breath between the answers—you will essentially fail to maintain a positive tone of voice. Try to use more words rather than less, remember where you are in the Sales Process, and keep in mind what you want your tone to convey. As we will discuss later, the words you choose will also affect your tone.

Conveying the correct tone and body language at the correct times requires you to be self-aware. You are on stage when you are with customers. They have never seen your performance, and they want it to be a good one. Therefore, you need to pay attention at all times to what your body language, tone, and words are conveying. Be cognizant of your stance, your hand and facial gestures, and your tone of voice. I once listened to a sales consultant use the word *fantastic* eight times in a three-minute span, when the sales consultant was speaking with a customer. If you use certain words or say *um* or similar interjections a lot, be aware that you do so, and when you are about to say such words, simply stop talking. The first step in being self-aware is to have someone record you or give you feedback on what you say and how you speak with your customers. Be self-aware!

## Words

The words or vocabulary you use will determine whether you are executing a transaction or creating an experience. Now, I know you thought that after high school, you would never have to worry about vocabulary again. Well, you were wrong. However, I am not suggesting that you use SAT words. What I recommend is that you should pay attention to the words you use and that you should try to use better words. While we will uncover what using better words entails in our chapter on Questioning Techniques, let me provide you with an example. When a customer calls us and sets up a time to visit our dealership, we refer to this as an appointment. I think we can use a better word. First, most of the places that people make appointments for are places they do not want to visit (e.g., dentists, repair facilities, and doctors). Conversely, places we make reservations for are places we do want to visit (e.g., hotels and restaurants). Therefore, we need to start using the word *reservation* in our dealerships rather than *appointment.* In the past we have used words that are negative, so it should not be too hard to start using more positive language. For example, dealership employees invented the term *the box* to describe the F&I office. By the way, it should come as no surprise that customers have always been reluctant to go to the F&I office. Who would want to go to the box? We will uncover more examples of poor vocabulary and better words to use in the chapters that follow. *I want to mention one more thing: to avoid confusion, I will continue to use the word* appointment *throughout this book.*

# CHAPTER 6

## LISTENING SKILLS

Listening is not hearing. Hearing is an ability we are born with. Listening is a skill that we need to develop. To elevate the customer experience, you need to get to know your customers. Listening will allow you to do this. In addition, not listening is the easiest way to get customers to not trust you and, ultimately, to not buy from you. Bruce Freeman, president of ProLine Communications, said that "people do business with those who take a sincere interest in them and listen to what they are saying they want and need. Clients who feel like they are being listened to feel accepted and appreciated. They feel like they are being taken seriously and that what they say matters."

Someone is listening to every sound you hear. When you walk outside, you hear birds chirping, and bird watchers actually listen to birds to determine the types of birds. When you walk through the shop area in your dealership, you may hear engines running. Your technicians are listening to the engines to understand the cars' malfunctions. In other words, the difference between listening and hearing is *understanding*. When you listen, you should try to understand what the other person is saying. Listening is not a passive activity; it takes a tremendous amount of concentration to truly comprehend what a person is trying to say.

When you are listening, listen not only to customers' words but also to their tones. Their tones will tell you whether they trust you, whether they had poor experiences elsewhere, whether they are confused, or whether they are confident—as well as numerous other things. Listen to their words and to *how* they say those words. It is easy to just listen to the words that customers say without trying to understand how they are saying those words. However, ignoring your customers' tones will not help you sell them cars today, let alone in the future. You need to enhance the customer experience, so you need to listen to what the customers' tones are conveying. To truly listen, you need to make sure you do a few things.

The first thing is to be quiet. You should not multitask while trying to listen. If you are talking, you are not listening. You have two ears and one mouth, so I suggest you listen twice as much as you talk. Perhaps you became a sales consultant because someone told you that you had the gift of gab, but the reality is that if you want to be a great sales consultant, you need to stop talking and start listening. Next, you need to eliminate any distractions. I know that dealerships are full of distractions (I never said listening would be easy); however, to truly listen, you must put aside all distractions. Doing so may require you to change locations within your dealership or to just block out extraneous noise. Also, keep in mind that if you are thinking about previous customers or about something that recently happened at your home, then you will be distracted and will stop listening. Your cell phone will also distract you, even if it only vibrates for a moment.

During such distracted moments, you may miss key things that your customers say. For example, imagine that a single male customer is in front of you and says, "We are interested in an SUV," but when he begins to talk, your cell phone vibrates, distracting you, so you miss the important pronoun he used. Then you proceed with the Sales Process, but when he tells you at the end that he needs to talk with his wife, you become surprised and wonder why he made that comment. However, he had already implied that he was not the only one involved in purchasing a new car, when he stated the word *we* and had you not been distracted by your cell phone vibrating, you would have adjusted the Sales Process accordingly.

Finally, with body language, you can show customers that you are listening. When you look at customers and nod while they are talking, you convey that you are listening. Also, your taking notes will convey that what customers have to say is important enough to write down. This will make them want to tell you more.

Speaking of taking notes, the only way you will remember what customers tell you is by writing down everything. Have you ever been at a fancy restaurant where the waiters or waitresses do not write down orders and simply memorize what everyone says? I do not know about you, but whenever that happens, my anxiety goes up, and I will be stuck wondering whether my food will be properly cooked.

The last thing you want to do is to increase your customers' anxiety. Remember that their anxiety is high just because they are at a dealership, so there is no need to exasperate their concerns. If, during the Presentation Step, you forget to go over a feature that a customer mentioned to you earlier (because you did not take notes or forgot what the customer said), the customer will not trust you. In that situation, you are not elevating the customer experience. Since most note-taking happens during the Needs Assessment, we will discuss how to take notes when that step is discussed. Before taking notes, you will need to ask permission to take notes. You will learn how to do this in the next chapter.

# CHAPTER 7

## QUESTIONING TECHNIQUES

You have probably heard the biggest misnomer in sales: "You could sell ice to Eskimos." People who are great sales consultants have often been told this. However, if you can sell ice to Eskimos, then you are not a salesman—you are a con man. You should not be trying to sell things to customers that they do not need. Great sales consultants first find out what customers need, and then they educate their customers on why their products will satisfy those needs. Great automotive sales consultants focus on finding out everything they need to know about customers by asking questions, and with that information, the automotive sales consultants determine which vehicles are best suited to their customers. Hence, the most important skill you can possess in sales is the ability to ask good questions. Notice that I stated "good questions." I am sure that everyone can ask questions, but if you want your customers to give you all of their important information—which is crucial not only for selling them a car today but also for selling them every car they will ever buy—then you need to ask good questions. Good questions are those that get you the information you need, and they should be asked at the right time and in the right way. Now, the right way means that the questions are asked using the proper vocabulary.

To elevate the customer experience, you must use the appropriate words. Retailers that enhance the customer experience all use the proper vocabulary.

## What to Ask

There are two types of questions that we ask when communicating with others: open-ended questions and closed-ended questions. The second kind may require yes-or-no answers, may be multiple-choice questions, or may be short-answer questions. With closed-ended questions, the person asking them usually has a good idea of what the possible answers are. Obviously, for yes-or-no or multiple-choice questions, the questioner knows exactly what the answers could be, and even for a short-answer question, the questioner should have a decent idea of what the answer will be. For example, the question "What time is it?" is a short-answer closed-ended question. While there are many possible answers to that question, I know that the answer (in hours and minutes) only has 1,440 possible choices (twenty-four hours × sixty minutes). Being the questioners, sales consultants have some idea of what the answers will be, which is why closed-ended questions get asked the most. Asking such questions probably originated from the idea that sales consultants need to control their customers. In other words, if you ask closed-ended questions, you must be controlling customers and the situations because you know what customers will probably say. The problem with this philosophy is that customers come into dealerships with their guard up. They do not trust you and quickly become anxious when you start asking questions. Their anxiety leads to an ironic situation in which customers hesitate to give you the information that will help you sell them cars. They end up giving you information in short answers only. In other words, when you only ask closed-ended questions, you are doing exactly what they want you to do. So who do you think is controlling whom? The only way you can reduce anxiety and elevate the customer experience is by asking more open-ended questions. The problem is that this is hard to do.

Now, I know you will not want to ask only open-ended questions. For example, when you ask a customer to buy a particular car, you want the question to be closed ended—you are not looking for a monologue, just a yes or a no. However, in most situations, especially during the Needs Assessment, the majority of your questions need to be open-ended. So let us discuss open-ended questions.

Open-ended questions are those that you do not know the answers to. These questions give you information that you will need to guide customers through the Sales Process. Many times, these questions are not actual questions but directives in which customers are asked to explain or describe something. Customers will still attempt to answer such questions, but they will do so with short and vague answers. Once again, their anxiety creates an ironic situation. Customers only come to dealerships because they need to buy cars, but they do everything they can to make it hard for you to sell them those cars. That is what happens after fifty-plus years of baggage.

Thus, you need to prompt your customers to give you more information by using words or phrases like *elaborate, tell me more,* and *go on.* Such phrases will encourage your customers to continue talking and to give you the information you need to sell them cars and to develop long-term relationships. When customers state something vague, you need to use drill-down phrases. For example, if a customer says, "Safety is important," do not just write down that the customer is interested in safety. The word *safety* is too vague, so you would need to ask a drill-down question. For example, you could ask, "Can you elaborate on what you mean by safety being important?"

Here is an example of what can happen if you do not drill down a vague term.

> A male customer says, "Safety is very important to me." You do not drill down. When you get to the Presentation Step, you discuss all of the safety features with the customer. While you are doing this, he looks confused, as though he never mentioned safety. The reason is...
>
> Let us rewind and handle the customer's comment in a different way. After he expresses his concern for safety, you respond by asking him to elaborate on what he means by safety. He then tells you that he feels that his current car is not safe. He says that when he merges onto highways, his current vehicle has poor acceleration, so he always feels as if he will get into an accident when merging into traffic.
>
> As you can see, what the customer considers to be a safety issue, you probably consider a performance issue. Since you did not ask an appropriate drill-down question, you end up discussing safety features during the Presentation Step, rather than performance features.
>
> Now you know why it is important to ask drill-down questions when customers state something vague.

Asking open-ended questions will assist you in elevating the customer experience in a couple of ways. First, the information you gather from customers by asking such questions will allow you to personalize the execution of each step in the Sales Process. Second, psychologists believe that if two people are having a conversation, the one doing all of the talking will have a higher opinion of the listener than the listener will have of the person doing all of the talking, even though the person doing all of the talking did not find out anything about the listener. The next time you are at a dinner party or barbecue and are seated next to someone you do not know, just listen. Ask a few open-ended questions, and let the other person do most of the talking. For example, say that you meet a man and let him do the talking. Later, when he is on his way home with his wife or girlfriend, he will probably start the following conversation:

"I met this great guy."
"Really? What does he do for a living?"
"I don't know."
"Where does he live?"
"I don't know."
"How many children does he have?"
"I don't know, but he is a great guy."

We all like people who listen to us. So if you want your customers to like you, all you have to do is listen to what they have to say. To get them to talk, you should ask them open-ended questions. If they like you, you will have elevated the customer experience.

## When to Ask

After you know what specific questions to ask, the next thing you need to determine is when to ask them. You will know whether you ask questions at the wrong time by paying attention to your customers' reactions. If customers' body language is closed off (crossing arms), if they physically get up to leave, or if their tones become more defensive, then you know you asked your questions at the wrong time. In some cases, customers may just be quiet.

The questions you ask at any given time need to be based on the cues your customers give you. Too often, we ask questions based on what information we need but fail to take into account customers' various behaviors. You will need to gather information from your customers in a logical manner. The questions you ask your customers must seem reasonable at the time. If your questions seem to come from left field, your customers will react accordingly.

For example, imagine that you are dealing with a female customer, and she says, "I am interested in an SUV." You, in turn, ask, "What are you currently driving?" This customer will wonder what prompted your question. It will not seem logical to her. This unusual question will make her anxiety go up, and her trust in you will go down. You need to get information in a logical manner and base your questions on what customers actually say. For example, if the same female customer says, "I am interested in an SUV because my current vehicle is too small," you can then ask about her current vehicle because she brought it up.

It is much easier to just ask question after question without taking into account what your customers are telling you. However, that way of asking questions is transactional. If you want to elevate the customer experience, then you need to ask questions in a logical manner and base your timing on the cues that your customers give you.

## Right Way to Ask

Perhaps the best way to elevate the customer experience is through the use of proper vocabulary. The words you use will speak volumes about the type of person you are and about the organization you work for. Using traditional car lingo will only increase customers' anxiety. When asking questions, your using the wrong words can hinder your ability to gather the information you need to create a great customer experience and to increase your customers' benefits of their doing business with you. Remember the Value Equation: everything you do and say has the potential to increase the Benefit. Your using the proper vocabulary will be a benefit to your customer, so the Value of doing business with you will increase.

A great example of the proper vocabulary to use for asking questions can be found in the restaurant industry. Imagine that you are at a casual-dining restaurant. At the end of your meal, your waiter directly asks, "Are you finished?" I want you to think about how that question sounds. Think about how a waiter who is at the end of an eight-hour shift would make those words sound. Now, in a five-star restaurant, a waiter asks you the same question but uses different words. In the five-star restaurant, your waiter asks, "Are you continuing to enjoy your meal?" The questions essentially ask the same thing, except the question asked at the five-star restaurant uses much better phrasing. Moreover, the words of the second question make it difficult to use a negative tone. In addition, the waiter who asked the first question sounds as if he or she wanted you to leave; the waiter who asked the second question sounded as if he or she wanted you to stay. The first question is transactional because it implies that you should simply pay up and leave. The second question is experiential because it uses the words *enjoy* and *continuing*.

Every question you ask can be asked better by using words that sound more pleasing to the ear. In most cases, this requires more words. An example from the car industry is a question that I am sure every customer who enters your dealership gets asked. This question, though it must be asked because you need the information it will provide, is often asked with wrong words. The question is, Have you ever been here before? Consider what that would sound like to a customer who had just walked in and had high anxiety about being in a car dealership. Moreover, if the sales consultant asking the question had been having a rough day and if his or her tone was not positive, those words could sound even worse. The experiential way to ask that question (i.e., the better way) would be to frame it in the following manner: Have we had the opportunity to serve you in our sales or service departments before? It would be tough to make this question sound bad, even if the person asking it was in a bad mood. Also, if you look closely at the words that were chosen, you will notice that I am suggesting that you inform your customers that you are there to *serve* them. The use of better vocabulary is how you begin to elevate the customer experience.

Earlier, you read that in order to increase trust and reduce anxiety, you need to tell your customers what is going to happen next and then to tell them the benefits of the next steps. This philosophy applies to the way you ask questions as well. When asking questions, consider telling your customers why you are asking the questions before you ask those questions. Too often, we ask questions, but the customers look puzzled or object. We then tell them why we need the information. To elevate the customer experience, tell your customers why you are asking certain questions. Also, make sure that the reasons why you ask certain questions are benefits to your customers. For example, I have heard many sales consultants ask customers the question, what are you currently driving? This question usually elicits the following response from the customers: "I am not trading it in." Now, the sales consultants were not asking the customers whether they wanted to trade in their vehicles. However, those sorts of responses stem from the customers' years of bad car-buying experiences. Instead, you could say, "In order for me to assist you better in determining your likes and dislikes for new vehicles, would you share with me what you are currently driving?" If you tell customers why you are asking them certain questions and if you explain the benefits of why you are asking those questions (to assist them better), you will elevate the customer experience.

Some of the questions you will ask will be closed ended, and if you do not use the proper words, your customers will feel as if they were being interrogated. One way to make your questions sound more conversational, especially with closed-ended questions, is to add a few words before the questions. Examples of these opening phrases, which are sometimes referred to as "cushions," are the following:

- "I am curious..."
- "I am wondering..."
- "If you don't mind my asking..."
- "In order to serve you better..."

Always remember that the vocabulary you use when speaking with customers is crucial to your long-term success—I cannot stress this enough. Concentrating on how you ask your questions will help you build benefits for customers, and as a result, they will come to value their experience at your dealership. Here are some examples of poorly worded questions and, where appropriate, the properly worded questions:

1. Who is the lucky person who will be driving this car? This question is condescending and typical of a hard Sales Process.
2. What features do you find most important? It is the sales consultant's job to determine this, which you will see in the chapter on Needs Assessment.
3. May I take some notes? A better way to ask this question would be to say the following: "In order to better assist you in selecting the perfect vehicle, would it be okay if I took some notes?"
4. Who are the decision makers? This question is a poor choice of words. Instead, say the following: "Pardon my

> curiosity, but who will be involved in the selection of your new vehicle?"

We will uncover more examples as we reveal each step in the Sales Process. For now, I hope that you see the difference between asking questions in the transactional way (which increases anxiety) and asking questions in the way that elevates the customer experience.

# CHAPTER 8

## THE SALES PROCESS

Today, all businesses create processes to achieve their goals. The car business is no different. For as long as I can remember, dealers have had a Sales Process. The goal of this process has been to sell cars. Make no mistake: the common Sales Process that most dealers have used has achieved this goal. The industry continues to sell millions of vehicles each year, and in most years, the industry sells more than the previous years. The problem is not the process but the execution of that process. Though dealers continue to sell millions of vehicles, remember the DrivingSales.com study mentioned at the beginning of this book and what it revealed: auto sales could rise about 25 percent if the retail experience improved. Just as the differences between casual-dining restaurants and five-star restaurants are not in the process but in the execution of those processes, the differences between average sales consultants and dealerships and exceptional ones are not in the sales processes but in the execution of those processes. The execution of the Sales Process has to turn the transaction of buying a car into an **experience**. This starts with changing the goal of the Sales Process.

While the goal of every individual action that dealership associates take is to increase the likelihood of their customers' doing business with them today and in the future, the goal of the Sales Process is not just to sell a car but to *provide customers with experiences that will compel them to buy cars at your asking prices, come back for their next cars, and refer their friends.* We will discuss in detail how to execute each step in the process, but first let me describe each of the steps. For a few reasons, these steps should sound familiar to those of you who have been in the car business awhile. First, remember that I mentioned that the issue is not with the Sales Process itself but with the execution of it. Second, I like to keep things simple. Therefore, instead of changing the name of each step, I will use phrases that we are all familiar with. So here are the steps of the Sales Process:

- Prospecting: I will reveal what you should do to make customers aware of you and to get them to come into your dealership.
- Greeting: We all know the expression "You only have one chance to make a good first impression." I will show you the best way to do this.
- Needs Assessment: This is the step where you find out what customers would need, want, appreciate, and so forth, in their next vehicle. This is the most important step in the process.
- Presentation: I will show you how to get customers so excited about the vehicles at your dealership that they will buy them at your asking prices.
- Demonstration: As we have all heard before, 90 percent of people who have not done a test drive will not buy the relevant vehicles, so I will teach you how to get all of your customers to go on demonstration drives.
- Trade Appraisal: This anxiety-producing step can be executed much better, as you will see.

- Asking for and Getting the Sale: In this chapter, I will describe not only how to prepare and present a proposal but also how to negotiate and overcome objections, and I will show you how to do both in ways that do not increase anxiety.
- Financial Services: I will reveal the best way to introduce your customers to the F&I manager.
- Delivery: This step needs to be a catalyst for your increasing the likelihood of your customers doing business with you *in the future.*
- Follow-Up and Creating Customers for Life: I will describe how you can get your customers to purchase all of the vehicles they will ever buy, from you.

As we look at each of these steps in detail, you will learn how to use the skills and techniques revealed in previous chapters to turn the transactions of buying cars into unforgettable experiences. You will see how to build the benefits in the execution of each step so that Value increases for your customers. Nothing happens in a vacuum. Each step builds on the one before it. The easiest way to have the entire process divert into a transaction is to try to only execute one or two steps as outlined. All steps need to be executed with the overriding goal of increasing the likelihood of customers' doing business with you in the present and in the future. If the Greeting is executed properly, then the Needs Assessment is easier. If the Needs Assessment is executed as an experience, then the Presentation will be better, and so forth. As you will find out, executing the Sales Process in a way that elevates the customer experience is hard. I make no apologies for that. However, the concepts are not difficult to grasp, and if executed properly, they will make you more successful than you ever thought possible.

Before we move on to the first step in the Sales Process, I want to discuss a concept that has influenced the Sales Process more than any other concept, and that is the notion of *control.* Managers often tell their sales consultants that they need to control their customers. As I mentioned, this concept of control has created sales consultants who pull their customers through the Sales Process in very transactional ways. The result is that there are more unhappy customers, and the ironic thing is that sales consultants never actually manage to control customers. However, I do want you, as a sales consultant, to control the Sales Process. I mean that you need to be the one who determines what is going to happen next. However, you need to do so in a way that makes customers feel that they are in control. You can do this by guiding your customers through each step in the Sales Process. You should move your customers from one step to the next in a logical way, one that does not produce any anxiety. Moving your customers through the Sales Process without skipping steps is imperative. The only way to create great experiences for your customers is to guide them through each step. Keep in mind that your providing great customer experiences is in customers' best interest.

If you use the proper words, body language, and tones, your customers will move easily through each step in the Sales Process. As they move from one step to the next, you will reveal the benefits of all that you have to offer. The execution of the process described herein actually ensures that customers will want to move from one step to the next. The more experienced you become at incorporating the concepts discussed in this book to executing the Sales Process, the more you will be able to *script the entire Sales Process in advance.*

The highest level of sales skills involves sales consultants' ability to script the entire Sales Process before it actually occurs. Skilled sales consultants accomplish this by thinking ahead as they uncover information about their customers.

As your customers provide you with their likes, dislikes, driving habits, and so forth, you should determine how you will use the information later on in the Sales Process. For example, imagine that you have a male customer who mentions during the Greeting that he almost got lost while getting to the dealership. In this case, you should make a note to discuss navigation with him during the Presentation. If this same customer also complains about how his back is bothering him, you should make a note to discuss the comfortable seating and lumbar support during the Presentation or Demonstration. What you are essentially doing by making such notes is scripting the rest of the Sales Process, so you will know in advance how you will guide him through the rest of the process. Obviously, your having a script would benefit you, and it would also benefit your customer because you are personalizing the Sales Process. Such scripts will allow you to be more efficient and will create personalized experiences for your customers.

# CHAPTER 9

## PROSPECTING

I bet that you are thinking that prospecting is old school. Well, yes, it is. Prospecting is also something that all successful sales consultants do. First, let us define it. Prospecting is what sales consultants do to reach out to potential customers to entice them to purchase certain products. Though dealerships can and should support this activity, sales consultants are the ones who ultimately perform prospecting. Dealerships implement marketing and advertising strategies to attract customers and to get them to buy vehicles. Marketing is broad and not specific; it is more of a transactional stratagem. Prospecting, on the other hand, is detailed, nuanced, and experiential.

New sales consultants should be spending the majority of their time on prospecting. More experienced sales consultants spend the majority of their time cultivating relationships with customers to whom they have already sold cars. This topic will be explored in detail in the chapter on Follow up and Customer Retention. For the most part, dealerships' advertising strategies promote the low prices that the dealerships offer. When we looked at the Value Equation earlier, we saw that one way to increase Value is to reduce price. By advertising the lowest prices, your dealership is attempting to increase Value. Ultimately, you can spend your day selling cars to people who were enticed to come to your dealership because they saw your low prices in the local newspapers, or you can attract customers to visit your dealership to buy cars from you. Customers who enter your dealership and ask to see you will spend more money and will be easier to sell to. Let us look at how you can attract these customers. Keep in mind that like everything I ask you to do, the execution of the Prospecting Step is hard. However, the concepts are not difficult to grasp.

Since you are a sales consultant, you need to think of yourself as a brand. All brands (e.g., McDonald's, Coca-Cola, and Chevrolet) put together marketing plans that let consumers know what the brands are and why consumers should buy their products. The newer brands need to spend more time on describing what they are to consumers; on the other hand, established brands do not need to spend much time on describing themselves to customers. Hence, Chevrolet does not need to focus on explaining what it is; however, a newer brand like Tesla does need to focus on explaining what it is. All brands, whether new or old, need to let customers know the reasons they should buy the brands' products. These reasons are the benefits of their products. The most successful brands show customers why the features of their products match what the customers are looking for in those types of products or services. These two aspects, what and why, are exactly what you will need to describe as well. Just as any other brand does, you need to let customers know about you and why they would be interested in using you to facilitate car purchases. To accomplish this, first determine what characteristics of sales consultants are most important to customers. Based on my research, I believe those characteristics are the following:

1. <u>Knowledgeable:</u> Sales consultants must be experts about the products and services they sell.
2. <u>Trustworthy:</u> Sales consultants must be trustworthy.

3. Genuine: Sales consultants must be genuinely concerned about whether customers purchased the best products for their needs.

Once you know how to express these characteristics, you will need to let potential customers know that you possess these characteristics. You will do so by developing a Marketing Plan. Keep in mind that just as a brand will first convey the benefits of its products through its advertising and marketing strategies, the ultimate determinant of whether or not customers purchase its products is determined when customers experience the benefits for themselves. For example, an automotive brand can advertise the great performance of its products, and doing so will attract customers interested in performance to look at the cars; however, if a customer determines that a vehicle's performance is poor after test driving it, he or she will not buy the vehicle. So if you promote yourself as knowledgeable, trustworthy, and genuine, you better back up those characteristics when your customers come into your dealership.

Customers want sales consultants to have certain characteristics (knowledgeable, trustworthy, genuine, etc.) because those qualities make the car-buying experience more pleasant. If you decided to purchase a product that was half of your yearly income, you would want the experience of buying that product to be enjoyable. But how does this relate to prospecting? Well, prospecting is to put a Marketing Plan together, to execute that plan, and to reinforce what you promote in the Marketing Plan when your customers arrive at your dealership.

The development of your Marketing Plan will consist of a few topics:

1. Background: This is the "who you are" section. You will need to let people know who you are and what you do for a living.

2. Benefit: This is the "why me" section. You will need to let people know why they should purchase cars from you. Keep in mind the characteristics that customers are looking for in sales consultants.
3. Medium: This is where you determine the most effective means of communicating with your potential customers. The first step in this section is to identify where you can find potential customers.

## Marketing Plan

Your Marketing Plan will be your prospecting road map. Without a road map, you will not know if you are headed in the right direction or when you arrive at your destination. In addition, by having a Marketing Plan, you will know what you need to do to prepare to execute the plan. John Wooden, the former coach of UCLA's men's basketball team and winner of ten national championships, said, "Failing to prepare is preparing to fail." Preparing takes work. However, it will make the process of prospecting much easier. As you execute your Marketing Plan, you must track and measure your successes and failures to fine tune your prospecting efforts. Finally, your Marketing Plan must be written or typed so you can refer to it easily and make changes as necessary.

## Background

This is the section in your Marketing Plan in which you tell people who you are, what you do, and where you do it. Always remember that you need to use the proper vocabulary and that you need to state everything in a way that reinforces the characteristics of being trustworthy, knowledgeable, and genuine. When you describe your story, mention your family, your hobbies, and all of the organizations that you are involved with. People trust others with whom they have things in common. If you state such things as where you went to school or the age and activities of your children, you are bound to hit on things that potential customers have in common with you, and when you do, they will place more trust in you. In addition, mention any training and education that you have had—especially automotive training and customer-service training, both of which will reinforce your knowledge and expertise. The best way to communicate all of this information is in a story rather than in a list. We will discuss storytelling in more detail later, but suffice it to say that people remember stories. You want your potential customers to remember you, so describe your background in a story. For an example of this, read the paragraph at the beginning of this book, where I describe my background.

This section is also where you let people know that you are a sales consultant and why you chose to be one. Make sure that you discuss the need to make the industry more customer friendly, and mention that you like to work with people and that you love cars. Also, discuss your dealership. Do not just say, "I work at ABC Motors." Tell everyone what is great about ABC Motors. Does your dealership donate to different charities? Is it involved in helping the community? Such activities reflect that your dealership is filled with genuine employees. Also, mention all of the services and amenities (free car washes, loaner vehicles, a great waiting lounge, etc.) that your dealership provides. Such things are benefits that will increase Value.

## Benefit

This is where you get to tell people about why they should buy cars from you. This is your Marketing Message, with which you differentiate yourself from other sales consultants. The best way to differentiate yourself is by using quotes from current customers. The main characteristics that customers look for in sales consultants need to be expressed with examples. The examples lend credibility. Any sales consultant could easily say that he or she cares about customers, but real quotes are priceless, whether they describe how a sales consultant seemed genuinely concerned about how a vehicle would be used or how the sales consultant never pressured a customer into a purchase. Another way to show your knowledge and that you genuinely care is to post third-party reviews of different brands of vehicles and aftermarket products. By posting (we will talk about where in the next section) good and bad third-party reviews of products, you show people that you are looking out for their best interests. Customers will respect and like you for doing so. Remember that you want customers to say that you are not a typical car sales consultant.

## Medium

The medium you use to reach potential customers with your Marketing Message will depend on where they are located. Keep in mind that the *where* does not have to be a physical location; it can also be a virtual location. Before determining where to find potential customers, we need to define them. A potential customer is someone who might be interested in one of your vehicles, has the means to purchase a vehicle, and has the time to proceed through the Sales Process. A potential customer can have all the money in the world and really want one of the vehicles you sell, but if that customer does not have the time to go through the Sales Process, then he or she is not a prospect. Moreover, as we will discuss, the Sales Process can and should be personalized for each customer, but each customer still needs to go through the process. On the other hand, a customer who is interested in one of your vehicles and has the time to go through the Sales Process but cannot afford it is also not a prospect.

You will find potential customers in the places that you frequent. These places include where you go physically and where you go virtually. Here are some examples:

- Your children's activities (sports, dance, clubs, school functions, etc.)
- Sporting events
- Religious organizations
- Fraternal clubs or similar organizations
- Businesses that you frequent (drycleaners, restaurants, etc.)
- Social networks like Facebook and LinkedIn and other online groups

Essentially, anyone you know and the people involved in the places you visit are potential customers.

Once you have a list of where to find potential customers, the next step is to determine how to reach those people and how to persuade them to visit you at your dealership. Depending on the potential customers, this may be achieved through the following mediums:

- Mail (old-fashioned "snail mail")
- E-mail
- In person
- Telephone
- Social media

The potential customers themselves will determine not only the most effective ways you can communicate with them but also the forms that the messages are sent in. Here are some Best Practices that sales consultants have used:

1. On their personal websites or on social networks, such as Facebook or LinkedIn, some sales consultants post their personal backgrounds and the benefits of doing business with them. Other topics that get posted include the previously mentioned reviews, information on customer service, and even famous quotes. Since you want customers to view you as an automotive expert, you should include insight into the car industry by providing links to interesting articles. (The power of links is that you do not have to write as much.) You can also include links to or screenshots of your customers' positive comments about you. Also, on your site, include videos of your vehicles, your dealership, and you.
2. Since video is so popular today, take advantage of it. Have someone use your cell phone to record a video of you in front of either cars or your dealership while you discuss your background and the benefits of buying cars from you. Upload this video to YouTube and include it on your main website. Also, by uploading the video to YouTube, it will create its own URL address. You can use this link in any e-mails you send to potential customers. Also, by visiting a QR-code-creator site, you can create your own QR code. Here is an example of a QR code that I created. Reading it with a QR-code reader will open my website, www.wrightautopro.com.

3. A QR code that you create will be linked to your video or to your website. If you put your QR code on the back of your business cards, then potential customers will have not only your contact information but also a video of you as well. Videos create credibility and help people to trust you because of the transparency inherent in the videos.

Finally, track how your customers hear about you and why they decided to visit you. In time, you will learn which prospecting efforts are working and which are not. Either change your prospect methods or discontinue them as you see fit.

# CHAPTER 10

## GREETING

The Greeting is when customers get their first impressions of you. As the saying goes, "You only have one chance to make a good first impression." Is visiting your dealership the most hectic part of your customers' days or is it a place of calmness that promotes decision making? After all, you are asking customers to purchase a product that is, in some cases, about half of their yearly incomes. As I uncover the best ways to greet your customers, I want you to keep a few things in mind. First, nonsales consultants may be the ones who initially greet your customers. However, nonsales consultants' actions will influence how customers feel about you and your dealership, which will affect your income. Therefore, you might want to have them read this chapter. Second, remember that all of the actions taken during the Greeting are done to increase the likelihood of customers' doing business with you in the present and in the future. According to the Value Equation, exceptional Greetings are benefits to customers and will build Value. If Greetings are not beneficial to customers, they will continue to focus on prices. Great Greetings get customers thinking about things other than prices. You want customers to think that your dealership is not typical. Proper Greetings will make the rest of the Sales Process easier and more efficient. Finally, the actions and suggestions that you will read may make you think of a luxury car dealership. This is the traditional way of thinking. The way luxury relates to the automotive industry has changed. First, if someone is spending over $25,000 for a product, I think that he or she probably considers it to be a luxury product. Second, you can buy a "luxury" Mercedes-Benz for $30,000 and a "nonluxury" Chevrolet pickup truck for $60,000. I believe that most customers will want exceptional experiences when purchasing either one. The Greeting is when you let customers know that purchasing vehicles from you will not be simple transactions, instead you will be elevating their experiences.

The surveys we revealed disclosed how customers do not like visiting car dealerships. In other words, when customers do visit your store, their anxiety is probably high. The Greeting needs to be designed to help them lower their anxiety and increase their trust in you. If customers' anxiety remains high, you will *not* increase the likelihood of their buying cars from you. To make the Greeting benefit customers, we will need to examine everything that happens during the Greeting, even those things that dealerships' management have control over.

## Pulling onto the Lot

When customers drive onto your dealership's lot, how are they greeted? Yes, the Greeting starts before they speak to anyone. What does your signage look like? Is it easy to navigate your lot and determine where to go? How are the signage and lighting on your lot? Do the customers need to spend ten minutes looking for places to park? Think about how that would influence customers' anxiety. Do you even know how long parking takes? Do you have valet parking? Think about how that would influence trust and benefit your customers. Wouldn't valet parking make your customers think that your dealership is not typical? All of these aspects have a major influence on how your customers will interact with you when they enter your dealership. In general, when consumers are not happy with something at a business, they tend to use price as the way to "even the score." It is consumers' way of increasing Value (go back to the Value Equation).

After your customers park, who greets them and how? Does rain or snow or similar weather change the Greeting? Think about how valet parking or greeting customers at their cars with umbrellas can make the transaction of parking into an experience for your customers.

## Entering the Dealership

The transactional way of being greeted when a customer enters the dealership is pretty basic. For example, the greeter says hello and asks how he or she can help the customer. Customers will usually state that they are interested in particular cars, and the greeter informs them that a sales consultant will be with them momentarily. In many dealerships, customers wander around the showrooms before they are greeted by sales consultants, who then ask them a few quick qualifying questions. Examples would be, have you ever been here before? and, what are you interested in? These are very transactional questions that do not reduce anxiety. By the way, when customers are in your showroom and looking to purchase an expensive product, where are their coats? This is a rhetorical question—I know that they are either wearing their coats or holding them. Think about that. You are allowing your customers to walk around uncomfortably because they are wearing their coats, and then you expect them to purchase your vehicles at your asking prices. Good luck with that.

As best-practice ideas are revealed for the Greeting, please think about how each affects customers' anxiety or trust and whether each action would increase the likelihood of customers' doing business with you. The following is the best practice for making what could be the transaction of being greeted and turning it into an experience. The customer pulls onto the lot and follows the signage to the valet parking area. The customer is greeted by the valet and handed a bottle of water. The valet says, "Welcome to ABC Motors. My name is John. In case you are thirsty, here is a bottle of water. We have other refreshments inside as well. While you are with us, may we have the privilege of washing your car?" As the valet walks the customer inside the dealership, he has a conversation with the customer by asking, "I am curious about your drive. Did you have any difficulty finding us?" After they enter the dealership, the valet introduces the customer to the receptionist. On rainy days, the valet has an umbrella. Now, I know what I just described is not possible at many dealerships, but think about how these actions would affect your customers.

Whether or not customers are greeted first by valets, the customers will enter dealerships at some point, and in many cases, receptionists will greet them. Before greeting customers, receptionists should check their lists of appointments to see if the customers are expected. After receptionists introduce themselves and get the customers' names, receptionists should ask the following question: Have we had the opportunity to serve you in our sales or service departments before? This question sounds so much better than, have you ever been here before? If a customer has made an appointment, the receptionist should say, "John is expecting you. Please, give me a moment to let him know that you have arrived." The receptionist then should call and inform the sales consultant that the client is in the showroom. This entire process, from the greeting made by the valet or receptionist to directly handing off the customer to the sales consultant should not take a long time. It should take only a few minutes.

Remember that the use of proper vocabulary is a benefit to customers and that as benefits go up, so does Value.

Sales consultants need to make sure they continue the experience for the customers by using proper vocabulary as they greet the customers. After introducing themselves to customers, sales consultants need to use very conversational tones of voice, as if they were speaking with people who have been invited over for dinner. Therefore, do not say, "How are you?" Instead, say, "Mr. Jones, how is your morning so far?" If your receptionist forgets to do it, ask to take a customer's coat and hang it up in your closet for guests' coats. Give the customer a slip, as they do at restaurants, so the customer knows that his or her coat will be taken care of. Use the Greeting as an opportunity to build rapport and establish trust by having a lighthearted conversation with the customer. Keep in mind that the information customers provide during these conversations is important. Whenever customers are talking, they are giving you information that will help you increase the likelihood of their doing business with you, so pay attention.

## Appointments

Before we transition from the Greeting to the Needs Assessment, I would like to discuss customers who have appointments to see you. We just uncovered how receptionists should greet customers with appointments, so let us go over what you can and should do to create great experiences for customers after you make appointments for them to visit you. The best way to provide great experiences to your customers is to concentrate on benefits. Doing so will create great experiences, and it will also increase Value (see the Value Equation). A benefit to the customers is that they have a sales consultant whom they trust, someone who genuinely cares about their concerns. The best way for you, as a sales consultant, to express this is by getting to know as much as you can about your customers. Robert Cialdini, the author of *Pre-Suasion: A Revolutionary Way to Influence and Persuade*, says that "it's that they [customers] want to deal with someone who likes them and who is like them. People trust that those who like them won't steer them wrong." The best way to have someone like you and to be like them is to find something in common. When your customers are in front of you, find commonalities through visual clues (sports caps, college rings, etc.). If you have known a customer for years, then you already know what you have in common. The commonalities you share with customers encourage them to trust you, leading them to feeling comfortable doing business with you, and such comfort and trust are powerful motivators that will get customers to seek you out for their future purchases of cars. In the twenty-first century, you can find these commonalities before customers arrive at your dealership.

With the Internet, you can see a tremendous amount of information about the customers who have appointments with you. You should access this information to help you find common ground with your customers and to help you make the dealership experience great for them. For example, you Google a female customer the night before her appointment and you find out that she attended the same college as you did. Well, you obviously should not say, "I Googled you last night, and I saw that we went to the same college." Instead, what you would do in this situation is wear a pin or a tie or have a mug with your college logo on it. If you do any of these things, your customer will probably say, "I went to that college too." Since you and the customer went to the same college, her trust in you would increase. Also, the customer will feel more relaxed and have less anxiety. You will have made it a better experience for her.

Ultimately, the reason to do this kind of research is not because you want to spy on your customers but because you want to serve them in the best way possible. Your customers will benefit if they feel more comfortable doing business with you. If the benefits increase, Value will grow too, as well as the likelihood of customers' doing business with you. Ultimately, what you are doing is turning their visits to your dealerships into experiences.

## Transition to Needs Assessment

Perhaps the most difficult task that you will have to do is what I insist happens next. If you truly want to elevate the customer experience, the Needs Assessment MUST happen sitting down with customers at a desk or table. Let me reiterate this: you must be sitting down with customers to do a proper Needs Assessment. You most likely do your Needs Assessment while standing by a car. This is not efficient and ultimately wastes customers' time. First, you cannot take proper notes while standing, which means that you will miss information that can help you later in the Sales Process. Second, if you are standing by a car, a customer will focus on the car, not on the questions you are asking. Third, if while looking at the car, you gather information and determine that the car you are inspecting is not the right fit for the customer, then you have wasted his or her time. Here is a news flash: people do not like their time being wasted. Finally, the goal of the Needs Assessment is to gather information that you can use throughout the Sales Process—specifically, information you can use to wow your customers during the Presentation. If you are by a car while doing a Needs Assessment, then you are combining the Presentation and Needs Assessment Steps, which means that you are concentrating on the transaction, not on the experience, and you will not increase the likelihood of the customer's doing business with you. Which brings us back to the transition from the Greeting Step to the Needs Assessment Step.

The transition is hard to execute because your customers do not want to sit down with you. Though we know that customers are at your dealership because they need to buy cars, their anxiety is so high that they will probably push back on everything that you do to help them find suitable cars. I know the situation is ironic, but customers' instinctive mistrust stems from the historical way that automotive sales consultants have manipulated their customers. Their sitting down with you is in their best interest, but they do not know this, so they will resist whatever you try to do. How you handle this resistance will determine how successful you will be as a sales consultant, so I want to provide some techniques you can use; however, these techniques are not tricks. You must learn to use your words and body language to transition customers into what is in their best interest. This will be hard.

# CHAPTER 11

## NEEDS ASSESSMENT

The Needs Assessment is the most important step in the Sales Process. During the Needs Assessment, you gather crucial information from customers and use it throughout the Sales Process to personalize the customer experience. Online sales companies, especially clothing companies like Trunk, use algorithms to determine customers' needs rather than send the same things to everyone. When applying for jobs, people research the relevant companies so that they know how to tell the employers why they, the applicants, are the perfect fit for the relevant jobs. When selling cars, you need to do the Needs Assessment so that later you can present to your customers why the selected vehicles are the perfect fits for them. In addition, a recent JD Power study concluded that "having a salesperson who completely understands the needs of the customer is far and away the single most impactful Key Performance Indicator, which speaks to the importance of having salespeople who can ask the right questions and then follow through on requests." Hence the reason that the skill to ask good questions is so important to elevating the customer experience. Within the next few pages, we will delve into how to use the questioning techniques revealed earlier when executing the Needs Assessment, but let us start at the beginning of this step.

The Needs Assessment begins in earnest after you sit down with a customer. I know you will be gathering information throughout the Sales Process, but the heart of finding out your customers' needs and wants for their next vehicles happens during the Needs Assessment. After greeting a customer, you should say, "Mr. Jones, to better assist you in selecting the perfect vehicle for your needs, I would like to gather some information from you. Let's have a seat over here, and by the way, may I get you something to drink?" As you say these words, use a conversational tone, and walk toward your desk or a table. This is the one time in the Sales Process when you will tell customers what is going to happen next and the benefits of the step (How to Build Trust), but do *not* ask for their permission. The reason you will not ask for permission is that the customers do not yet fully understand the benefits, so they will say no if you ask for permission. Therefore, just make a comment like the one above and walk. The key is to ask them questions like, "May I get you a drink?" The customers will walk with you as they answer these types of questions. Essentially, what you are doing at this point is guiding customers through the Sales Process, and doing so requires you to be firm but polite. No matter what, though, customers must be sitting down with you when you do the Needs Assessment.

Okay, I know that there are going to be instances in which customers give you some resistance, so you need to know what to do and say. Here are some scripts you can use for some of the common objections to sitting down. In each instance, your body language (walking as you are talking) and tone (firm but polite and conversational) will not change.

- A customer says, "I just have a few questions, so I don't need to sit down." The sales consultant says, "Mr. Jones, I would be happy to answer all of your questions, in order to better assist you, I would like to get some information from you first. Let's have a seat. By the way, may I get you something to drink?"

- A customer says, "I don't have a lot of time." The sales consultant says, "Not a problem, Mr. Jones. Let's have a seat and discuss what you would like to accomplish while you are with us. By the way, may I get you something to drink?"
- A customer says, "I just want a price on..." The sales consultant says, "Mr. Jones, I would be happy to assist you with that. In order to better serve you, I would like to get some information from you. Let's have a seat. By the way, may I get you something to drink?"

In all of these scripts, the sales consultants are always stating that whatever they are doing is to better assist the customer.

If customers enter your showroom and walk over to certain models and tell you how excited they are to see those cars, you should *not* calm them down by having them go to your desk. You want customers who are excited about your vehicles. Allow these customers to go see the cars. When they start to ask you questions about those cars, ask them to join you at your desk so you can gather information that will help you assist them in selecting the correct vehicle and equipment. Once you are sitting down with these types of customers at your desk or a table, execute the Needs Assessment. To elevate the customer experience during the Needs Assessment, you need to execute the process by using the skills and techniques referenced earlier in this book.

Once you are seated with a customer and, perhaps, he or she is enjoying a drink, you should begin the Needs Assessment. To start, you need a few items. You should have plenty of business cards, and you should give a customer one when you sit down. Obviously, you need to have a pen and a notepad to take notes.

Now, please look professional. Buy yourself a nice leather or faux leather padfolio which contains a notepad and a pen. I have seen sales consultants use Post-it notes, three-by-five-inch pads, and clipboards. If you use any of these items, consider what you are communicating to your customers. Elevate the customer experience by being professional. In addition to giving customers your business cards, you should also give them a small notepad and inform them that you are providing the notepad and pen in case they would like to take notes. This shows that you are transparent and that you are not hiding anything. Before taking notes, you need to ask to take notes. As you read in the chapter on Questioning Techniques, there is a proper way to ask this question. Do not say, "Do you mind if I take some notes?" or "May I take notes?" The customer may answer yes to these questions but then may wonder why you need to take notes. Customers' anxiety is high at this stage, so do not make it go up further. If you ask a customer to take notes and he or she says, "Why do you need to? I am not buying today," then you may assume that his or her anxiety is definitely rising. The better way to ask to take notes—the way that increases the likelihood of customers' doing business with you—is to frame the question in the following manner: "To assist you better in selecting the perfect vehicle, it would be helpful if I took some notes. Would that be okay?" Framing the question in this manner will help to put the high-anxiety customers at ease. They will relax a little and have their drinks and wait for you to ask your questions.

When asking questions, you need to use a conversational tone. If you have a list of questions that you want to ask and if you ask them one after the other, then your questioning will sound like an interrogation, not a conversation. If you interrogate your customers, the customer experience will not be elevated. The questions you ask need to be based on the cues the customers give you. Therefore, you should not have a list of questions that you need answered; you should have a list of information that you need to gather. For example, if a customer says, "I really like your xyz model," do not say, "What are you currently driving?" That question will not make sense at that time. Rather than have a list of questions, you need a list of information that you need to gather. This list needs to be broad enough so that you can tailor your questions to your customers. Here is the list of information that you need (this is very broad, so feel free to add to it as you see fit):

- Hot buttons or benefits: safety, performance, comfort, appearance, and so forth
- Vehicle needs and wants: what customers must have in their next vehicles and what they would like to have
- Time frame: such circumstances as whether the customers have leases due soon or whether they have children going to college in the near future
- Budget: you need to be assured that the customer can afford the vehicle he or she is interested in.
- Current vehicle information: what they like and do not like about it
- Driving habits: how will they use the vehicle (*You are interested in how they will use their new vehicles in the future, not how they currently use or used to use their vehicles. These ways might be the same or might not be.*)
- Customers' knowledge about your dealership and your vehicles: both will help you guide your discussions
- Personal information:
  - Who will be driving the vehicle
  - Who will be purchasing the vehicle
  - Who will be involved in the selection of the vehicle
  - Rapport-building opportunities
    - Sales consultants should always be listening for opportunities to build relationships with

customers by paying attention to any personal information that customers provide. Their doing so will build trust and elevate the customer experience. It will also provide you with information that you can use later in the Sales Process. The best way to make a transaction into an experience is through establishing a personal connection. Customers have no desire to build rapport with you, so you need to look for opportunities to build rapport. For example, imagine that you are helping a female customer who says, "I need space in the back for my son's football equipment." Do not begin by immediately discussing cargo space. Instead, ask her about her son's football experience. Then make a note that her son plays football and that a particular amount of space is required, and remember that you will use this information during the Presentation. In this way, you have begun to *script the Sales Process.*

If you gather customers' information from all of these categories, then you should be able to eliminate any objections other than the typical business-deal objections, such as price, payment, and trade value. A list of these categories can be on a piece of paper in your padfolio.

Since the Needs Assessment is all about asking questions, let us look at some questions you might ask. First, before you ask a question, always keep the end in mind. For example, let us say that you know your vehicle's navigation system is easy to use, so if some customers mention that they do not like the navigation systems in their current vehicles, ask them what they do not like about those navigation systems. If they say something similar to "it is hard to use," you will use that information during the Presentation and Demonstration. Do not start by immediately telling your customers about your vehicle's navigation systems—you are still doing the Needs Assessment not the Presentation. Second, do *not* ask customers what features they want in their next vehicles. Questions that focus on that topic are asked often but are terrible questions. The minute that customers state the features they want, you better make sure that your vehicles have them. Once customers verbalize the features they want, they will feel compelled to obtain those features. This means that if your vehicles do not have the desired features (even if your vehicles have better features), customers will use that fact to either not buy the relevant vehicles or ask for lower prices.

Next, technology is changing so quickly that your vehicles may have features of which customers are unaware. So to some extent, your asking them what features they want is irrelevant. Also, it is your job to find out what is important to your customers (e.g., how they use their vehicles) and to take that information and match it up with the features of your vehicles and to educate your customers as to why the features on your vehicles will benefit them. Your educating customers will occur during the Presentation. So do not ask them what features they want. Here is what you should say instead:

- "So that I can assist you properly in determining what you would like and not like in your new car, may I know what you are currently driving?"
    - "I am curious about something: what do you like most about your current vehicle?"
- "If I may, can you tell me what about the performance that stands out to you?"
- "Please, would you tell me about how you plan to use your new vehicle?"
    - This is better than just asking, "SUV or car?"

These questions are drill-down questions. You should use drill-down questions in response to customers' comments. For instance, if a customer tells you that safety is important, you need to realize that statement is vague. When customers make vague comments, you need to ask a drill-down question like, "Could you elaborate on what you mean by safety being important?"

The question that you will most likely use at the beginning of the Needs Assessment is something like "I am curious what brought you in today." Customers will respond with comments like "I am interested in a *model X*." You should respond with something like "I am wondering what interests you in the *model X*." If you make such comments, you will allow customers to give you information that you can use to guide the conversations.

Here is another example. If a customer says, "I need to look at your *competitor's model Y*," you would respond by saying, "Many of our customers compare our vehicles to *model Y*. I am curious about something: What is it about *model Y* that interests you?" Once again, you are basing your questions on what the customer has said. Doing so will be logical to the customer. Also, as you read earlier, customers will often give you vague information; I know it does not make sense. Customers do not want to be at dealerships; the only reason they go there is because they need to buy cars. Yet they will do everything they can to make it more difficult to sell them that car, including giving you short responses and vague answers to your questions. To get customers to give you the information you need, you must use drill-down phrases such as *go on*, *elaborate*, and *tell me more*. You must continue to use such phrases to guide your customers through the Needs Assessment, and your doing so will ensure that you get all of the information (based on the categories listed earlier) that you need. Once you have all the necessary information, you will then proceed to the Presentation Step.

# CHAPTER 12

## TELEPHONE TECHNIQUES

Before proceeding to the Presentation Step, I would like to spend a chapter discussing a tool that you should be using not only to increase sales but also to improve your customers' experience. The telephone may seem very old school, but it is not. First, here is some background information. Back in the '70s, '80s, and '90s, the telephone was used extensively to get customers in the door. Dealerships spent a tremendous amount of time, money, and energy training sales consultants on how to use telephones to encourage customers to visit the dealerships. Then the Internet was invented, and everything changed. Dealers believed that customers were going to use the Internet and not the telephone to contact dealerships. Therefore, all the time and money that was spent on telephone training moved to Internet lead generation and training. This strategy proved to be the right choice. From the late 1990s until about 2012, the majority of customers contacted dealerships via the Internet, not through telephones. However, things started to change in 2012. That change was the invention of the iPhone.

In 2015, phone calls outpaced e-mail or form leads by a 4:1 ratio. From 2014 to 2016, phone leads were up 46 percent versus Internet leads. Customers were starting to call their dealerships again. The invention of the iPhone was a game changer in that regard. Today, most car buyers carry smartphones, and using a click-to-call phone link is easier and quicker than filling out information forms on websites or sending e-mails. In addition, most people use their smartphones more than any other devices to access the Internet. On such a relatively small screen, to scroll through a website for information becomes difficult and time consuming. Just calling a business is much easier and quicker than visiting the relevant website. Hence, if your dealership tracks sales calls, you will most likely find that the number of customers calling your dealership has grown and continues to increase each year. The problem dealerships face is that many of them either have cut way back on telephone-skills training or are continuing to train sales consultants to use telephones as if the year were still 1985. By the way, it is not 1985, 1995, or even 2005—heck, it is not even 2015 anymore. Therefore, you need twenty-first-century telephone skills. Fortunately, you are about to learn what those skills are.

I would like you to stop reading for twenty seconds. Stop reading and take the break. Okay, now that you are back, I want to ask, "Did you make a phone call during the twenty-second break?" I am guessing that you did not because you did not have enough time. Now, I want you to think about the businesses you call in your daily life. Like most people, you probably call restaurants, doctors, barbershops, hair salons, and so forth. You call these businesses because you either want to do business with them or already do business with them. What do these topics have to do with the sales calls that you receive? Well, if customers call you, you can assume either or both of the following: First, the customers have time to talk; otherwise, they would not have called. Second, they are interested in doing business with you.

The reason these are true is because they are true for all of us and for the places that we call. Since many dealerships receive more sales calls than customer visits, it would appear that the reason the customers are not coming in is due to something the dealerships did or did not do when customers spoke with them.

In the historical use of telephones, they were considered to be tools used to get customers into dealerships. I believe that customers who call you are already in your dealership. They are just there virtually rather than physically. In today's world, when customers contact your dealership or you contact them via telephone, e-mails, Skype, or FaceTime, they are at your dealership. They are just there virtually. This concept changes how you use the telephone as a tool to communicate with your customers. Let me explain by showing you two examples.

First, the historical way: *just get them in*

| | |
|---|---|
| Sales consultant: | "Hello, thanks for calling ABC Motors. How can I help you?" |
| Customer: | "I am interested in obtaining information on a new X." |
| Sales consultant: | "X is a great car. We are currently having a sale that only lasts two more days. When would you like to come in and look at X?" |
| Customer: | "I can come in tomorrow at two o'clock." |
| Sales consultant: | "Great, see you then." |

Okay, I know that the conversation would include a little more information, such as the customer's name, telephone number, and so forth. However, the reality is that the historical way of speaking on the telephone was very transactional—just say whatever you need to say to get the customer to come in. By stating that the dealership is having a sale, the sales consultant is trying to build Value immediately by lowering the cost. That is not something you should be doing. Also, once the customer comes in, the sales consultant will have to perform the Needs Assessment with the customer.

Now, consider that the customer calling the dealership is already in the dealership in the virtual sense. Rather than just trying to get the customer in, the sales consultant begins the Sales Process on the telephone. This requires a better greeting and a proper Needs Assessment.

The new way: *here virtually*

| | |
|---|---|
| Sales consultant: | "Good morning. Thanks for calling ABC Motors. This is John." |
| Customer: | "Hi, John. My name is Fred, and I am interested in obtaining information on a new X." |
| Sales consultant: | "Fred, the X is a great car. In order to better assist you, it would be helpful if I asked you a few questions. Would that be okay?" |
| Customer: | "Sure." |
| Sales consultant: | "First, I am curious what encouraged you to call our dealership?" |

The sales consultant would then continue to gather information from the customer just as he or she would execute the Needs Assessment if the customer were physically in the dealership. Once you have a good idea that a certain car is the best vehicle for the customer, you would set up an appointment for the customer to come in and look at and drive that car. When the customer arrives, the exact vehicle he or she is interested in will be pulled out and ready for the Presentation and Demonstration.

As you digest both scenarios, I would like you to answer this question: Which of these scenarios increases the likelihood of the customer doing business with you? Also, the second way is more experiential. The telephone call is a better experience, and when the customer arrives, you can tailor the Presentation and Demonstration because you have found out information about the customer, information that you can use to create a better experience for him or her. Finally, by doing the Needs Assessment over the telephone, you reduce the time the customer has to spend in your dealership. Remember that customers' anxiety will be lower when you talk on the telephone rather than in person. If they do not like you or what you are saying, all they have to do is hang up their phones. In person, they need to physically leave, which is more uncomfortable; hence, they experience more anxiety in person than on the telephone. Finally, to really make sales calls great experiences for your customers, you need the assistance of everyone who answers the telephone.

Once again, the historical way of answering the telephone is a transaction, in the sense that someone answers phone calls and blindly transfers customers to sales consultants. Consider the following example:

Receptionist: "Thanks for calling ABC Motors. How can I help you?"
Customer: "I would like to speak to someone about a new X."
Receptionist: "Please hold while I transfer you to a sales consultant."

The receptionist will then either page a sales consultant or transfer the call to a sales consultant blindly (meaning the sales consultant will answer the telephone and will immediately speak with the customer). If the customer tells the receptionist any information, it will be lost and will have to be reiterated to the sales consultant. This might sound familiar, and you now know why you have more sales calls than customers visiting your dealership. By the way, the historical way of answering the telephone does not increase the likelihood of the customer doing business with you today or in the future.

The better way of answering the telephone is for the receptionist to gather some information from the customer and then transfer the call to a particular sales consultant.

Consider the following example:

| | |
|---|---|
| Receptionist: | "Thank you for calling ABC Motors. This is Jane." |
| Customer: | "Jane, this is Lisa. I would like to speak to someone about a new X." |
| Receptionist: | "Great! I am curious about something: Have we had the opportunity to serve you in our sales or service departments before?" |
| Customer: | "No, I have never been there." |
| Receptionist: | "Okay, may I place you on hold while I locate a sales consultant?" |
| Customer: | "Sure." |

Receptionist then calls a particular sales consultant and provides him or her with the information about the customer and asks if the sales consultant can take the call.

| | |
|---|---|
| Receptionist: | "Lisa, thanks for holding. I am going to transfer you to Rick. He is one of our top sales consultants, and he can assist you and answer all of your questions. Once again, thank you for calling ABC Motors." |
| Customer: | "Great." |
| Sales consultant: | "Hello, Lisa. This is Rick. I understand that you are interested in a..." |

Consider the customer's anxiety level between the two scenarios. Which type of call would reduce anxiety? Which would increase the likelihood of the customer doing business with the dealership? Finally, I would like to review the greeting to make sure that you picked up on something. The best practice for greeting your customers is *not* to say, "How can I help you?" The best practice is to say, "Good morning. Thanks for calling ABC Motors. This is [your name]." Do *not* say anything after your name. Do not ask whether you can help or assist your customers. Remember this: *anything after your name erases your name.* Your customers will remember the last thing you said. If you would like them to remember your name, then do not state anything after you say your name. Also, this will help you get their names because they will most likely state something like, "Hi, [your name]. This is [customer's name]." Finally, there is no reason to ask customers how you can help them. Of course you can help them; otherwise, you would not have answered the telephone.

Once a telephone call with a customer is over (hopefully it ended by scheduling an appointment for the customer to visit the dealership), grab a colleague and go to the vehicle that you will be presenting to the customer when he or she visits. Have your fellow sales consultant record a video of you in front of the vehicle. As you talk into the camera or smartphone, first thank the customer for speaking with you (use his or her name), spend two to three minutes doing a quick review of the vehicle (especially if it is preowned), and quickly provide your background and experience. Take this video and e-mail it to the customer, and thank the customer in writing for speaking with you. Mention that you look forward to seeing him or her on whatever day and time you both decided on. By doing all of this, you will change the thank-you e-mail from a transaction into an experience.

I could write an entire book on the proper use of the telephone, but for the sake of this book, I just wanted to provide you with a new way of looking at a great tool you can use to turn transactions into **experiences**.

# CHAPTER 13

## PRESENTATION

The Presentation Step in the Sales Process is the fun step. Why is it fun? This is where the sales consultant gets customers so excited about a vehicle that they will buy it at MSRP. If sales consultants are not upbeat, positive, and enthusiastic, then customers will not become excited. No one wants to buy a car from Debbie Downer. Now, I know you are thinking that no one is going to pay MSRP. Well, I can guarantee you that if you do not think your vehicles are worth MSRP or if you do not ask for MSRP, then you are correct—no one will pay MSRP. You need to believe your vehicles are worth MSRP and show customers why. Therefore, the goal of the Presentation Step is to show your customers the features of the selected vehicles and how those features are benefits to them. The only way you can do this is if you first do a proper Needs Assessment to find out what is important to them. Once again, each step builds on the one before it. The way to express excitement to customers is by envisioning yourself pulling a white sheet off a car and saying, "Ta-da!" when the vehicle is revealed. While you are thinking these words, you will actually say, "Mr. Jones, because of what we have discussed, I believe this vehicle is perfect for you. Let me show you why."

Another point I want to make is that when your customer pays MSRP or any other amount for your vehicle, he or she is not just paying that amount for the vehicle. The customer is also paying for the positive experience that you have provided. If you execute your Sales Process as a transaction, then the price that the customer pays will be only for the vehicle. However, if you execute your Sales Process by turning every transaction into an **experience**, then the price that your customer ultimately pays for your vehicle—whether he or she pays MSRP or something else—includes more than just the car.

In an ideal scenario, you will do a presentation using the exact vehicle that the customer is interested in. However, this is not often possible or feasible. Therefore, many sales consultants will do presentations by using vehicles in their showrooms. In either case, the Presentation progresses the same way. Sales consultants execute the Presentation *not* by telling everything they know to customers but by concentrating on a few of the features and benefits that the customers will find valuable. Sales consultants specifically do this by discussing the features that the customers mentioned during the Needs Assessment. If sales consultants discuss all of the features, then they waste their customers' time. *This is an important point and may be different from what you have been told or from what you are currently doing.* The historical way of doing a presentation is the six-, eight-, or ten-point walk around, in which sales consultants start at the driver-side doors and walk around the vehicles while going over every feature. However, the sales consultants—by concentrating on the features instead of the benefits—build *no* Value. In addition, these sales consultants are creating transactions in which their customers only hear them say, "Blah, blah, blah, blah…" Sales consultants also waste customers' time by discussing things that the customers are not interested in. If you want to save your customers time, then execute your presentations better.

Many sales consultants spend too much time discussing certain features because they have not done their homework. Albert Einstein said, "If you can't explain it simply, you don't understand it well enough." Make sure that you know your products inside and out and that you can anticipate any questions your customers may have. Also, if you have a solid grasp of your vehicles' features, you will have an easier time articulating and showing your customers those benefits.

Historically, sales consultants have been told to get customers to say yes five times. Some automotive sales consultants believe that if their customers say yes several times, then the customers will convince themselves to buy the relevant cars. I always find it interesting that many people in the automotive industry think they are psychologists. I prefer you to get your customers to say wow as many times as possible. Every time customers utter such interjections, you can safely assume that the benefits are increasing, and if the benefits go up, so does Value. Let us find out how to get customers to say more positive interjections.

## What, Why, and How

During the Presentation Step, sales consultants describe WHAT the features are and WHY they are benefits to the customers. HOW features work is explained during the Delivery Step and possibly during the Demonstration. Too often, sales consultants start telling customers how certain features work. When you go to buy a refrigerator, you need to know that it has an ice maker, and during the Presentation, the sales consultant will point out the ice maker. If you tell the sales consultant that you like crushed ice and if the refrigerator makes crushed ice, the sales consultant will also point this out. However, during the Presentation the sales consultant does not need to bother explaining how it makes ice (whether crushed or not). After you purchase the refrigerator, then you will need to know how it makes ice so that you can set it up properly, but you do not need that information during the Presentation.

In addition, customers' questions can be used to transition them to the Demonstration. For example, if a customer asks, during the Presentation, about how the back-up camera works, the sales consultant will mention that how it works will be shown during the Demonstration. As another example, during the Presentation, a sales consultant tells a customer that the liftgate of a vehicle can be adjusted to a certain height so that it will not hit the top of his or her garage. During the Presentation, the customer does not need to know how to adjust it, just that it can be adjusted. The *how* will be explained during the Delivery.

## Five Wows

An ordinary sales consultant Tells. A good sales consultant Explains. A great sales consultant Inspires. Be a great sales consultant by getting your customer to say wow multiple times. How? By telling a Benefit Story. Let us revisit the Value Equation: Value = Benefit – Cost. The Presentation Step is the main step where you increase the Benefit by showing customers why the features of your vehicles are benefits to them. Once again, by getting to know your customers during the Needs Assessment, you can personalize the benefits. To make the benefits look as if they were on steroids, tell Benefit Stories. A Benefit Story brings a benefit to life for a customer. Research has shown that people remember 65–70 percent of the information shared through a story and only 5–10 percent of the information conveyed through facts and figures. Everyone loves a story; that is why we go to the movies, read books, and watch television shows. When we were little, we often said such things as "feed me" and "tell me a story." Maryanne Elsaesser, a real-estate agent, uses stories to sell houses. She could say that a house has three bedrooms, one bathroom, and an eat-in kitchen, or she could say, "With magical, embracing arms, this home can whisk you right back to your childhood. Remember yourself racing down the street with your brand-new Schwinn bike, and you are greeted by the smell of bacon frying for your special BLT lunch." Let us face it: everyone knows that the house is a three-bedroom, one-bath home. Therefore, a real-estate agent needs to trigger the other senses.

The realtor Barbara Ostroth says, "Instead of saying large backyard, you could say deep yard, great for BBQs, to help buyers imagine their families enjoying the property." *Adweek* found that storytelling helps make hotel rooms worth more. In an *Adweek* study, participants were shown an online picture of a hotel room, and a typical description (square footage, size of the bed, air conditioning, etc.) accompanied that picture. Another group of participants were shown the same picture, and only this one was accompanied by a picture of a guest and a story of when that person stayed at the hotel. The room paired with the story was worth 5 percent more. The same study found similar results with wines that had a story about the winemaker versus one that did not. Stories increase benefits, which increase Value.

I am sure you have told a customer that a vehicle has heated seats, only to have him or her ask you ten minutes later about whether the vehicle has heated seats. However, what if you had said the following instead: "This past winter, I went ice skating for the first time in twenty years. It was one of those very cold days, but my kids wanted to go, so we went. Needless to say, I spent a lot of time on my behind because I had not skated in years. By the time we were done, I was freezing, especially my behind. When we got into the X vehicle to come home, the first thing I did was to turn on the heated seats. I have to tell you that I was amazed at how quickly the seats heated up, even when the temperature outside was below freezing." Customers remember this kind of story, but this particular one would only work if you drove the same vehicle that the customer was interested in and if the customer was interested in seats that heated up quickly. Now, you would have found out that the customer was interested in seats that heated up quickly during the Needs Assessment. Perhaps the customer complained about the heated seats or lack thereof in his or her current vehicle. You made a note of the comment, and the information was used during the Presentation. Instead of just saying that the heated seats heat up quickly, you told a story. When the story was finished, the customer responded with a "wow."

The best Benefit stories are the ones where you get customers to imagine themselves using the relevant vehicles. In the past, sales consultants were told to have customers take mental ownership of the vehicle. The historical way of doing this was through using tricks. For example, after a demonstration drive, the sales consultant might say, "Park in the sold line." Conversely, the best way to have customers take mental ownership is by using words that create stories in which the customers imagine themselves using the vehicles.

For example, during the Needs Assessment, you discover that your male customer has difficulty pulling out of parking spaces at the mall. Now, you could say that the vehicle he is interested in has a rear cross-traffic alert that will warn him when a vehicle is behind him or about to be behind him, or you could tell a story that would bring this feature to life for him. That story would go something like this:

> Mr. Jones, imagine you are at the mall, and as you walk out to your vehicle, you notice a large van at one side of your car and a truck on the other side. You get into your car, start it, put it into reverse, and begin backing up. You are hoping that no one comes flying by, because the two

> large vehicles are preventing you from seeing the oncoming traffic. As you back up, a warning light appears all of a sudden and an audible sound warns you to brake because a vehicle is coming up behind you. You don't even see the other vehicle in the back-up camera screen, but your car has warned you. You are safe because you are driving the model X, which has a rear cross-traffic alert system that warns drivers of vehicles coming up from behind. I will show you how the alert system works during the Demonstration.

As you read the story, you imagined a car backing out of a parking spot at a mall. When you tell your customers such stories, they would imagine themselves backing out. That is how you get customers to take mental ownership of the vehicle.

If you just give your customer facts and figures, you will reduce the Presentation Step to a transaction. Storytelling, however, inspires and creates an experience for your customer.

# CHAPTER 14

## TRANSITIONS

Before we move on to the Demonstration Step, I would like to discuss two topics that do not fall neatly into any of the Sales Process Steps. For lack of a better title, I decided to go with "Transitions" because what we will now discuss usually happens between steps.

### Dealership Tour

At some point during the Sales Process, sales consultants need to perform dealership tours with their customers. During this tour, sales consultants will point out everything that makes their dealerships great (e.g., amenities or a great service lounge). While revealing everything that makes your dealership fantastic, remember to use the information your customers provide during the Needs Assessment to personalize the tours and to increase the benefits. For example, if customers tell you that they hate to sit around and wait for their vehicles to be serviced or if they mention something about how they hate to waste time, then point out your alternative transportation options (e.g., loaner cars and shuttles). Conversely, if some of your customers mention that they always wait while their vehicles are being repaired, then discuss all of the amenities in the service waiting area (e.g., refreshments and Wi-Fi). By concentrating on your dealership's "features" that are important to your customers, you will be increasing benefits. By the way, storytelling works here as well. For instance, you could say that your dealership cleans every car that comes in for service, or you could tell a story. Here is an example:

> Mr. Jones, last week a customer whom I sold a car to was in to have that car serviced, and after she picked up her car, she deliberately came into the showroom to find me. She told me that when she brought her car in, it was so dirty because of the bad winter weather that she could not even tell what color it was. She then expressed her appreciation for how spotless her car was on the outside, and she was amazed that all of the Cheerios that were all over the back seat had been cleaned up as well. Mr. Jones, when you have your car serviced with us, we make sure it is returned to you much better than when you dropped it off—even if, as is the case with the first service, the car does not drive any differently.

Hopefully, Mr. Jones says wow after he hears that story. Use stories not only to build benefits but also to show your customers how the transaction of having their vehicles serviced will be an experience. Finally, the tour needs to be completed *before* the Demonstration. After arriving back from a demonstration drive, you will discuss with your customer all of the features that the customer loves about his or her vehicle. Customer's excitement does not need to be interrupted with a tour of the dealership. Finally, after a customer agrees to purchase a vehicle, another tour should take place. This one is specifically aimed at introducing the customer to the service department and scheduling his or her first service appointment.

## All Alone

At different times during the Sales Process, your customers will be left alone. It might be when you have to prepare vehicles for demonstration drives, it might be when their vehicles are being appraised, or it might be when you are getting numbers from your manager. In any of these scenarios, you have to ask yourself, "What is my customer doing while he or she is alone?" However, I already know what they are doing. According to a DMEautomotive study, 48 percent of car buyers are checking their smartphones while visiting dealerships. When visiting dealerships, about 30 percent of millennials look at the websites of dealerships' competition. So much for all the talk about "controlling customers." This is the equivalent of you saying to a customer, "Mr. Jones, I will be back in a few minutes. While I am gone, why don't you drive down to our competition and speak to them, and then come back. By that time, I will be ready for you." Obviously, you would not do that, but that is exactly what is happening—not physically but virtually. There is a better way to engage customers when they are left alone.

## Electronic Evidence Manual

The time customers are waiting for you to return, whether they are looking at their smartphones or not, is a transaction. As such, the time they are waiting is also a waste of your customers' time. As we discussed earlier with the restaurant example, time is not about minutes, hours, or seconds; it is about the value of time or the lack thereof. Sitting around is a waste of time, so customers will feel like the Sales Process is taking too long. Therefore, you must provide something for them to do while they are waiting for you. To make sure this activity is not a waste of time, it has to be somewhat entertaining and educational. In the past, many sales consultants have put together Evidence Manuals that they share with customers. In essence, the manuals are "why buy here and why buy from me" booklets. These booklets usually include other customers' testimonials and information about the dealership and the brand. Well, in the twenty-first century, booklets will not cut it. You need an electronic version.

An electronic Evidence Manual is simply a video presentation that educates customers about why they should buy vehicles from you and your dealership. First, this video can be developed using numerous online applications that allow users to put together presentations with screenshots, videos from the Internet, and videos that you have shot. One of these electronic Evidence Manuals could contain the following items:

1. A video of you introducing yourself and your experience
2. A video tour of the dealership
3. Screenshots of customers' testimonials from DealerRater, from e-mails you received, or from third-party sites
4. Videos that your manufacturer has disseminated

Ultimately, pretty much anything you want can be on this video. You can set it to music, and if you really want to be creative, develop a few with different lengths and, perhaps, ones that go into detail about different models, thereby allowing you to customize these videos for your particular types of customers.

The electronic Evidence Manual can be stored on your computer or tablet. When you are about to leave your customers alone and after telling them where you are going, you can hand them the tablet, hit play, and ask them to watch the video. The great thing about electronic Evidence Manuals is that they are a tool that increases Value even when you are not with the customer.

# CHAPTER 15

## DEMONSTRATION

After you finish your Presentation, it is time to go on a demonstration drive. The goals of the Demonstration are to educate customers about any features that need to be demonstrated and to have customers experience the vehicles. If the vehicles you use for the Demonstration are the ones that you just used for the Presentation, then the transition will be easy. On the other hand, if you, like most sales consultants, use a vehicle in the showroom for a Presentation but need to transition to the Demonstration, you will need to first reference a feature that you presented and will need to let the customer know that you will now be showing him or her how that feature works. For example, you could say, "Mr. Jones, now I would like to show you how helpful the rear cross-traffic alert can be by demonstrating it during our test drive." Second, you will use the tools and techniques you just read about in the chapter on Transitions.

According to an Autotrader study, 88 percent of customers will not buy a car without test-driving it first. Obviously, this makes sense. I do not know about you, but I would not buy a pair of shoes without trying them on first. By the way, when you try on shoes, do you try on those that are almost like the ones you want to buy or are exactly the ones you want to buy? You need to do a better job of making sure that customers test-drive the exact vehicles they want to buy. I know this is not always practical, especially if your dealership does have the desired vehicles. However, if the vehicle is not exact, then the Demonstration becomes a transaction.

If 88 percent of customers will not buy cars without test-driving them first, why would any customers object to taking test-drives? Take a minute to think about that. Keep thinking. Okay, some customers do not need or want to go on demonstration drives, and their reluctance is due to a couple of reasons. First, a customer might have already driven a particular vehicle. Second, a customer might have already owned several models of a particular vehicle, so he or she does not need to drive it again. These reasons are totally legitimate. If I owned a pair of black shoes and, after wearing them for six months, wanted the same pair but in brown, I would not need to try them on. If one of your customers has driven or owned a particular car model, you should have found this out during the Needs Assessment. Another reason customers do not want to test-drive certain vehicles is because they have decided those vehicles are not the ones they want. Once again, you should determine during the Needs Assessment or Presentation what your customers want. The only other reason customers would not want to test-drive vehicles is because they do not like you. They will not reveal that, of course. They will give other excuses. Once again, you should know this.

If the vehicle presentations are executed using the vehicles that will be demonstrated, then some of what we will discuss can be performed before the presentations. If the presentations are done on different vehicles, then you will need to perform some of this between the Presentation and Demonstration. By doing a Needs Assessment on the telephone, you can almost guarantee to use the same vehicle for both the Presentation and Demonstration. Much of what needs to be accomplished before the demonstration drives actually occurs and can be done while preparing for the customers who called and made appointments to come in. When your Needs Assessment is done in person, then your customer will be waiting while you perform these pre-demonstration-drive tasks. Hopefully, you have a great electronic evidence manual.

Every action we are now going to discuss needs to be thought of in the context of turning the transaction of a typical test-drive into the experience of a personalized demonstration drive. The personalization of the Demonstration is what will turn it into an experience. First, you need to have some predetermined routes that you will go on with customers. These routes need to showcase all of the possible driving scenarios that customers could find themselves in. Once you determine the driving habits of your customers (during the Needs Assessment), you can personalize the route so that it matches the customer's daily driving routine. Second, you want a vehicle to be set up exactly as the customer will have it after he or she purchases it. If possible, you want to do this beforehand or, at least, when you arrive at the car with the customer.

At the car, pair customers' phones to the vehicles, program their radio stations, and make sure the vehicles are heated or cooled depending on the weather outside. You want the customers to start imagining themselves owning the car; in other words, you want them to start taking mental ownership. Obviously, you will have needed to make copies of their driver's licenses, explain the reasons why you have to do so, and assure customers that their privacy will be protected. As the sales consultant, you will always drive first while the customer sits next to you in the passenger seat. If you take out a couple, ask who would prefer the front seat. This is very important. I know some of you do not drive. Let me explain why this is important. In my training classes, I ask a participant to hand me his or her phone. I then ask him or her to demonstrate the features. The first thing the participant will tell me is to push the button at the bottom of the phone, which I will do. The participant will then tell me to touch an app. However, in the couple of minutes that have gone by, the screen has gone dark, so the participant now needs to start over. I then give the phone back and ask the participant to demonstrate it. The participant will tilt the phone toward me so I can see it, and then he or she will start to show me how to use certain features. When the participant is done showing me, he or she will hand me the phone to try it. Well, that is what you will do by driving first. You will demonstrate the features that, based on the Needs Assessment, you feel will benefit the customer. So you might say the following: "Mr. Jones, you will notice that a vehicle is passing us on the right, and as you are about to see, a light will appear in the mirror to alert you to the car, which may be in your blind spot."

After driving and showing your customers some of the features that are important to them, you will stop at a predetermined location and turn off the vehicle. Offer the primary drivers the opportunity to drive first. Show them how to adjust the seats, mirrors, wheel position, and so forth, and then have them turn the radio to one of their preset stations. Then close the driver's door, and get back into the vehicle. If there is more than one customer on a particular drive, offer to ride in the back seat. Also, if more than one customer is going to test-drive a vehicle, preplan the next changeover location. While the customers are driving, ensure that the directions are clear and specific, and refrain from demonstrating additional features while they are driving. While they are driving, you should be quiet; only answer questions. One of the best practices is to have the customer go to the drive-through of his or her favorite coffeehouse (Starbucks, Dunkin' Donuts, etc.) and to treat the customer to a drink. Once again, you need to personalize the experience.

When you return to your dealership, have the customer park the vehicle next to his or her current vehicle. Ensure that the parking spot has plenty of room for easy parking and for walking around the vehicle (you need to set this up before leaving on the demonstration drive). By parking next to their vehicles, customers get to see the differences between the new vehicles and their older vehicles. Once you have exited the vehicle, stand next to the customer looking at the vehicle and ask, "Mr. Jones, now that you have had an opportunity to look at and drive this vehicle, I am curious, what do you like most about it?" Too many sales consultants ask, "Wouldn't you agree this is the perfect car for you?" or something similar. DO NOT ASK THIS! You need to ask a question that will get customers to say, "This is the perfect car for me." Even though customers may nod along and say yes repeatedly, they might not believe that it is the perfect car for them. However, if you ask the customer, "Now that you have had the chance to drive this car, what do you think?" By framing the question in this manner, anything positive that the customer says can be taken as he or she wants to buy the car. The customer could have said something negative, but he or she did not. Therefore, when the customer says something to the effect of "I like it a lot" or "I like everything about it," you now need to ask for the sale. This is as simple as saying, "Great, let's go to my office and do the paperwork." If a customer says, "Well, if the numbers work," the response you give, as you start to walk to your office, should be "Let's go make them work."

By the way, if you do a proper Needs Assessment, the only objections that your customer can provide at this point will be related to money. This includes financing, interest rates, and trade values. These are the only topics you have not discussed yet. The customer cannot say that he or she needs to speak to his or her spouse or look at other vehicles or any other excuses. The reason these excuses cannot be said is that you would have uncovered all of these concerns during the Needs Assessment and would have adjusted your process accordingly. If, during the Needs Assessment, the customer mentions that his or her spouse needs to look at the vehicle, you should consider whether going on a demonstration drive would be worth it. You might decide instead to take the vehicle to this customer's spouse. If you do go on a demonstration drive with this customer, you would not ask this customer to go inside and work on the paperwork after you returned to the dealership. You would ask the customer to take the vehicle to his or her spouse or something else.

One of the reasons that Questioning Techniques are so important is that you are using questions to guide customers through the process, and you will always know where you are going to end up. Finally, if customers do tell you that they need to speak to their spouses but if, during the Needs Assessment, they specifically stated they did not need to speak to them, the only logical reason they are bringing up their spouses is because they do not like you. As we already discussed, customers will not say they do not like you; they will come up with excuses. If this happens at this point, go and get your manager. Your manager is there to help you with these types of situations.

We will go with the assumption that the Demonstration Drive went well and that the customer is ready to go inside and talk numbers. This will bring us to our next step. Keep in mind that all steps build on the ones before them. If you do a poor Needs Assessment, the Presentation and Demonstration will be generic and transactional. However, if you execute all of the steps according to what we have revealed, customers will trust you, like you, and want to do business with you because you created experiences for them.

# CHAPTER 16

## Trade Appraisal

The trade-appraisal process is one of the most contentious steps in the Sales Process. It often increases the anxiety of both customers and sales consultants. The problem is that historically, this process has not been transparent, and customers believe they are being taken advantage of. This happens when you execute the Trade Appraisal process like this:

> A male customer tells you that he has a vehicle that he wants to trade in. You write down some basic information, get his keys, and give them to your manager. You then continue with the Sales Process. Your manager determines the value for the customer's vehicle, which is shared with him during the negotiation. Often, the actual number is not provided because it is just "part of the deal." When the customer does get the number, he objects to it, so the sales consultant is then put into the uncomfortable position of defending a number that he or she had no involvement in determining. This leads to a back-and-forth discussion with the manager, which makes this process an uncomfortable transaction.

However, the situation could be worse. The night before the customer visits your dealership, he or she might have spent thirty minutes online to determine the value of his or her vehicle. If your trade-appraisal process only takes ten minutes, the customer will put more value in his or her number as he or she wonders how you came up with your number. For example, imagine you have someone coming to your house to appraise it for a refinance. The appraiser knocks on your door, and when you open the door, the appraiser hands you his or her business card and leaves without looking inside your house. The appraiser takes only a quick look at the outside. When you finally receive the amount at which the appraiser valued your house, I am sure you would question the number because you would feel that the appraiser did not do a thorough appraisal. Well, your customers will feel the same way about your vehicle appraisals.

Before we unveil the way to make the Trade Appraisal an experience, I would like to mention a few other actions that are too often taken by sales consultants or managers. These actions can increase anxiety. First, many sales consultants will go out to customers' cars with the customers and do a "silent walk-around." In a silent walk-around, a sales consultant walks around a customer's car and points out flaws on the vehicle without actually saying anything. The idea is that the customer will see the sales consultant touch the blemishes and realize that the vehicle is not worth what he or she thought it was. In essence, silent walk-arounds demean customers. Are you trying to trick them? You are not a psychologist, so stop trying to pretend you know what a customer is thinking. A silent walk-around is not transparent, obviously, and it is transactional.

Next, do not ask your customer what he or she wants for his or her trade. The only reason you would do this is because you are hoping that the number he or she wants is less than what your manager will appraise the vehicle for. To use car lingo, you would be trying to "steal their trade." What other industry tries to steal from their customers? Perhaps if everyone did his or her job correctly, you would not need to steal from your customers to make money. In addition, once customers verbalize the numbers they want for their vehicles, they will protect those numbers. This means that they will feel they have to defend those numbers because they verbalized them. Ultimately, they do not want to lose face, so they protect the numbers. What someone thinks something is worth is not relevant to what it actually is worth. It is great that you think your house is worth a million dollars. After all, you are very attached to your house, and your kids grew up there, so of course you think it is worth a million dollars. An appraiser, however, would not care about such things.

You might be wondering why the Trade Appraisal chapter appears after the Demonstration chapter. Well, there is a reason: appraising customers' trade-ins should occur after the customers have agreed, provided all the numbers work, to buy your vehicles. If customers are not ready to buy today or are undecided about whether or not to buy your dealership's vehicles, then you should not appraise their trade-ins. The value of their vehicles will change; therefore, you cannot give them numbers until you know that they are ready to buy. Also, customers' trade-ins are part of the purchase transactions, just like customers' down payments; therefore, if a customer is not purchasing a vehicle, your dealership should not give the customer a definitive value for his or her vehicle. If you want to give a customer a ballpark number, that is fine, but do not give an appraised number. Just as you do not need to know if customers are putting $1,000 down or $5,000 down until they are ready to buy, you do not need to know if their vehicles are worth $1,000 or $5,000. Now, customers may want approximate numbers just for their own calculations. If that is the case, then here is what you should do. You need to educate these customers that the process for Trade Appraisals is time consuming and costly and that the appraised values can change because of market conditions. If your dealership is not busy, then you can go online with the customers and, using a guide like Kelley Blue Book, show the customers how to get a rough idea of what their vehicles are worth. Sales consultants should use house-appraisal analogies to help explain the process. Banks will only appraise houses if their customers are going to take out a mortgage with them. Also, banks charge customers for the appraisal, regardless of whether the loans ultimately get approved.

Turn the Trade Appraisal from a transaction into an **experience.** First, let us discuss responsibilities. At most dealerships, a manager is responsible for conducting trade appraisals and, ultimately, for determining the value of a customer's trade-in. Sales consultants are responsible for the trade evaluations and for educating customers on the process for trade appraisals. It is the sales consultants' job to educate customers as to why their vehicles are worth what the dealership states they are worth. Keep in mind that it does not matter what the dealerships down the street think the trade-ins are worth. What matters is what your dealership decides they are worth. Your educating the customers has to come *before* the appraisals take place. Also, the goal of the Trade Appraisal is to determine what customers' vehicles are worth to your dealership. To create a Trade Appraisal experience, everyone needs to understand the concept of Educate versus Defend.

In a typical Trade Appraisal process, you provide customers with values for their trade-ins and then defend how you determined that number. This straightforward process is transactional. The experiential way is to begin by educating customers on how you will determine the value and then to execute the process as stated. Sales consultants need to reveal to customers how their dealerships determine the values of trade-ins. A sales consultant must explain to a customer that the dealership's manager will do the following:

- He or she will look over the Trade Evaluations that the sales consultants and the customers have filled out.
- He or she will drive the vehicle to be traded in.
- He or she will look at some guides to determine what the customer's vehicle is worth. It is *important* to mention as many guides as possible—Autotrader, Black Book, Kelley Blue Book, Auction Reports, and so forth.
- He or she will take supply and demand into account. If your dealership has ten vehicles like the customer's and if they have not sold in thirty days, that fact will deduct value from the trade-in. Conversely, if your dealership recently sold five vehicles like the one to be traded in, that fact will add value to the trade-in.
- He or she will consider reconditioning costs and seasonality (depending on the vehicle and the dealership's location), and he or she will run a Carfax vehicle-history report.
- Once he or she is done with the above, he or she will determine the value of the vehicle, which he or she will share with the sales consultant, who will then share it with the customer.

The Trade Evaluations are what sales consultants fill out when they go with their customers to their vehicles. These are different than the Trade Appraisals for the following reasons:

- Sales consultants will go to the trade-ins with the customers and point out not only things that will add value to those trade-ins but also things that will deduct value from those trade-ins.

- Sales consultants must be open and honest. You are not hiding anything.
- Sales consultants have to build Value in the process for Trade Appraisals. Once again, if your customer spends twenty minutes online determining what his or her vehicle is worth and then your Trade Appraisal only takes ten minutes, the customer will put more value in his or her number.

The ultimate reason for doing Trade Evaluations is that when customers object to the numbers, which they will always do (by the way, if they do not, you have a problem: you do not want a customer to say, "Great, I was only expecting this amount..."), you can use the Trade Evaluations to help resolve those objections. We will reveal how to do this in the next chapter.

In addition to the Trade Evaluations, sales consultants will also gather information about the trade-ins from the customers. This information could include the following:

1. Has the vehicle ever been in an accident?
2. Has the vehicle been smoked in?
3. Do they have the title? Is there a lien on the vehicle?
4. Do they have the service records?
5. Do they have an extended-service contract?
    a. If the answer is no, sales consultants will educate the customers on how having this can add value to their trade-ins, and if the customers are interested in those types of contracts, the financial-services manager will discuss them later.

Additional information can be gathered as well and provided to the sales managers who perform the Trade Appraisals. Once again, you will notice that as customers provide you with information, you can continue to script the rest of the Sales Process (e.g., you can plan to talk about extended-service contracts).

One of the best practices for conducting Trade Appraisals is to provide customers with offers for their vehicles that will remain even if the customers do not purchase vehicles from your dealership. However, certain parameters for how long the offers remain good must be communicated. For example, offers can remain good for a certain number of days or for a certain number of miles driven. Moreover, sales consultants should tell customers that other dealerships will not provide such offers; by doing so, sales consultants build trust with their customers and Value for the offers.

# CHAPTER 17

## Asking for and Getting the Sale

Once the sales consultant has finished the Vehicle Presentation and Demonstration and has confirmed that the vehicle selected not only is the correct vehicle for the customer but also meets all of the customer's needs, the sales consultant will move to the next step in the Sales Process by asking the customer to purchase the vehicle. The Trade Appraisal will happen at some point during this step, depending on your dealership's process.

The responsibility for asking for the sale rests with the sales consultant. The preparing of the proposal to be presented to the customer is the responsibility of the sales manager working with the sales consultant. Once a proposal has been developed, the sales consultant will present it to the customer. I understand that at some dealerships, experienced sales consultants may do this entire process themselves. The goal of this step is to put together a proposal that takes into account everything the sales consultant has uncovered about the customer and to gain the customer's agreement to the proposal.

## Asking for the Sale

After returning from the demonstration drive and after having the customer explain what he or she likes about the vehicle, the sales consultant will ask the customer to purchase the vehicle. Asking the customer to buy the vehicle is as simple as saying, "Now that we have determined the best vehicle for you, would you like me to write up the buyer's order so that you can take the model X home?" The customer may respond with comments like, "If the numbers all work out." This means that they have agreed to buy the car, so all that the sales consultant has to do is make sure the numbers work.

After the customer confirms that he or she wants to buy the vehicle, the sales consultant will leave the customer and meet with the sales manager to review what has transpired with the customer, and based on the information that the sales consultant has gathered, the sales manager will put together a proposal that the customer will likely agree to. The numbers that are prepared must take into account information regarding the customer's budget and financing preference. For example, does the customer want to purchase a vehicle outright, or does he or she want to take out a lease? If the customer wants a lease, what sort of terms would he or she accept? Sales consultants should have uncovered such information during the Needs Assessment. If the numbers do not take such information into account, the customer's anxiety will increase, and the chances of selling the vehicle will drop.

With the proposal in hand, the sales consultant returns to the customer. The sales consultant must convey confidence through his or her body language and tone of voice that this proposal is one that the customer should be happy about.

As you read earlier, when sales consultants leave the customers to go to speak with the sales managers to prepare the proposals, the customers should be given tablets with the sales consultants' electronic Evidence Manual. Remember that 63 percent of shoppers use their mobile devices at dealerships. When they are alone in your dealership, you do not have control over them, so they are probably visiting third-party sites virtually. They are at the end of the process, and you need to reinforce their decisions to buy your cars; you do not want to let them second-guess those decisions while you are getting numbers. The electronic Evidence Manual and any other videos that you provide to the customers transform the transaction of waiting into an experience.

## Getting the Sale

After the customer has been presented with the proposal, the next step is to prompt a mutual agreement. To do this, the sales consultant must identify the customer's objections and dispel them. Then the sales consultant must use the information gathered during the Needs Assessment—as well as throughout the Sales Process—to educate the customer on why the proposal is a good one. Should the customer reject the first proposal, the sales consultant needs to focus on resolving the objections, which may mean preparing another proposal that is mutually beneficial. Some dealerships like to present a proposal that is based more on what the dealership would like rather than on what the customer wants. If your proposal does not align with the information that your customer provided to you, then you are making the presentation of the proposal into a transaction. The proposal presentation becomes an experience depending on how you present them (i.e., how you use such things as your body language or words can drastically change the texture of the presentations) and on how closely the proposal takes into account the information the customer provided. This does not mean that you should sell the vehicle at the price the customer suggests; it means that you should present a proposal based on the customer's needs and wants. Moreover, even if you do all of this correctly, you will still get objections from your customers.

Notice that I stated you *will* get an objection. Customers still prefer to negotiate (see the first chapter), so you will get some pushback when you provide your customers with proposals. The key for all of your negotiations is to end up closer to your numbers than to theirs. The information you gather from your customers will help you achieve this. Moreover, executing this step requires that sales consultants first identify customers' true objections. Doing so requires the use of skills that the sales consultants used earlier in the Sales Process—skills such as listening and questioning techniques. To identify customers' objections, sales consultants also require an understanding of the differences between excuses, objections, and reasons.

- *Excuses* are the customers' knee-jerk reactions, which are often comments like "I am just looking." Customers often give Excuses early in the Sales Process because they have high anxiety at that time. Also, customers use Excuses to protect themselves from being taken advantage of. As you execute your Sales Process by turning every transaction into an **experience**, hopefully your customers' anxiety will be reduced. If, however, they state Excuses during the negotiation process, you should assume that they do not like you. I know that we do not want to hear this. However, if you are honest with yourself and pay attention, being disliked will not come as a surprise. For example, you may present a proposal, and the customer may say something similar to "I need to speak with my spouse." However, you remember that during the Needs Assessment, this customer actually stated the opposite. What these conflicted statements imply is that the customer, for whatever reason, does not want to do business with you. In this situation, you must bring in your manager or another sales consultant. If you do not, you will lose the sale.

- *Objections* are the general statements that customers use to explain why they cannot continue in the Sales Process. The main Objections you usually hear revolve around prices, payments, trade values, and interest rates. Most of the time, you will not be able to resolve these objections because they will be stated vaguely. Just as we discussed earlier, if customers state things vaguely, you need to drill down. In the case of vague objections, you need to drill down to uncover the true reasons underlying the objections.
- *Reasons* are customers' explanations for why they cannot continue in the Sales Process. The Reasons are what you can resolve by educating your customers.

To identify whether customers' responses are excuses, objections, or reasons, sales consultants must first say Empathy Statements and then use drill-down questions. Empathy Statements are comments that convey to customers that you are putting yourself in their shoes. As soon as customers state objections, their anxiety goes up. Your response to those objections will determine whether their anxiety continues to rise (which would decrease the likelihood of successful sales) or stops rising (which would increase the likelihood of completing sales). Empathy Statements that sales consultants should say after customers voice objections ought to resemble the following:

- "If I have not fully explained the value in what we have to offer, we would never expect you to take advantage of it. Fair enough?"

- "If it does not meet your standards, we would not expect you to..."
- "If you are not comfortable, we would not expect you to..."
- "If it does not make sense, we would not expect you to..."
- "If you do not see the benefits, we would not expect you to..."

All of the examples above may start with the following openers or similar ones:

- "I understand..."
- "I appreciate your concern..."
- "Many customers raise that issue..."

When customers say something similar to "okay, that's fair," the sales consultants have permission to continue the conversations and to ask drill-down questions that will uncover the customers' reasons for their pushback. The drill-down questions should resemble the following:

- What makes you uncomfortable with [stated objection]?
- What makes you hesitant with [stated objection]?

After customers state their first reasons, the sales consultants will continue to ask questions to uncover all of the customers' reasons before trying to resolve any of them. For example, consider the following dialogue:

| | |
|---|---|
| Customer: | "That payment is too high." (This is an Objection that cannot be resolved.) |
| Sales consultant: | "Mr. Jones, I understand. If I have not fully explained the value in what we have to offer, |

| | |
|---|---|
| | we would never expect you to take advantage of it. Fair enough?" |
| Customer: | "That's fair." (Their anxiety should stop rising.) |
| Sales consultant: | "What makes you uncomfortable with the payment?" |
| Customer: | "The payment on my current lease is lower." |
| Sales consultant: | "Other than the fact that the payment on your current lease is lower, is there anything else that makes you uncomfortable with the payment?" |
| Customer: | "My friend just bought this model, and his payment is lower." |
| Sales consultant: | "Other than your current lease being lower and the fact that your friend's lease payment on their model X is lower, is there anything else that makes you uncomfortable with our lease payment?" |
| Customer: | "No, that's it." |

Now the sales consultant can resolve the Reasons.

Objections or roadblocks can come up at any point during the Sales Process. The technique described above can be used during any of the steps or whenever customers raise objections. If sales consultants properly execute each previous step in the Sales Process according to this book, then at this step, the only objections the customers will give will revolve around prices, payments, or trade values. Also, if customers state the reasons right from the start, then drill-down questions are unnecessary.

The next part of this step involves resolving the objections or, more specifically, the Reasons the customers give. This is accomplished by using the information that has been gathered from or shared with the customers throughout the Sales Process. Sales consultants need to be able to resolve customers' Reasons by educating customers with information that was already provided by the customers or the sales consultants. For example, if a customer objects to the value a dealership determined for his or her trade-in and if the Reason the customer gives is that Kelley Blue Book is stating a higher value, then the sales consultant needs to educate the customer by using the information shared earlier. For instance, the sales consultant should remind the customer that Kelley Blue Book is a great guide in determining the value of vehicles, and the sales consultant should also say that the dealership actually uses Kelley Blue Book and several other guides. As they discussed earlier, the dealership uses multiple guides to determine the value of the customers' trade-ins. The sales consultant should continue by stating that while Kelley Blue Book may be higher, there are other guides that the dealership uses, and the sales consultant should state those other guides. Then the sales consultant should say that those other guides have lower values than what the dealership determined the customer's vehicle is worth. It is important for the sales consultant to refer to the discussion that he or she had with the customer when determining the trade-in value, earlier in the Sales Process. This will lend credibility to the case the sales consultant is making.

As mentioned earlier, during negotiations, sales consultants are trying to close the gaps between customers' offers and the ones the dealerships disclosed. Using the information gathered from and revealed to the customers, sales consultants not only will be able to accomplish this but also will do so in an experiential way.

## Telephone Customer—Best Price

I would like to take a moment to uncover how to handle telephone customers, who often seem like customers with objections. I am referring to customers who say such things as "I just want your best price." First, do not assume they are looking for the lowest prices. These customers probably have no idea about how much the relevant models are listed for. I know that this is a stretch, but you never know. Do not make assumptions. Ask questions to find out what you need to know. Now, even if telephone customers are looking for low prices, their concerns are probably more about affordability or financing. Once again, use questioning techniques to find out. Also, be aware of your tone of voice on the phone. I have heard plenty of sales consultants' tones become negative the moment telephone customers ask for the best prices. As you are about to see, you can sell this type of customer a vehicle if you remain positive and use the correct words.

First, your answer to a customer who says something like "I just want your best price" should resemble the following: "I'd be happy to give you a price. To do that, I will need to ask you a few questions about the vehicle you are interested in—would that be okay?" Do *not* use *but* or *however*—just state very calmly what you need. Proceed to ask the customer the questions you learned about in the Needs Assessment chapter. By using those questions, you are starting the Needs Assessment and may get the customer off the best-price topic. Now, I know that the type of customer you need the most assistance with is the one who does not get off the best-price topic. Therefore, let us find out how to make this type of customer buy a vehicle from you.

The example I want to use is a telephone customer who says, "Here is the deal: I am calling three dealerships located near me and asking each one for their best price. I will buy a car today from the dealership that gives me the best price. I have been on each dealership's website, so I know all of you have the exact vehicle I want. The vehicle is a blue model X with an MSRP of Y." This customer then gives you the specific vehicle he or she is interested in. You now have a choice: give the customer a price or tell the customer what everyone else is telling him or her, which is, "If you come into our dealership, we will beat any price you get from our competition." Both choices are transactional in nature, and you are now competing on price.

Remember the value equation: Value = Benefit – Cost. The customer is trying to build Value by concentrating on the cost. If you give him or her a price, you have done the exact same thing. Concentrating on price is all about the transaction. You need to make this telephone call an experience. The way you do this is to change the dynamics of the conversation. If you do not like the way the story is unfolding, change it. Here is how:

After the customer reveals that he or she is calling three dealerships to find the best price for a vehicle, the conversation continues in the following manner:

| | |
|---|---|
| Sales consultant: | "Mr. Jones, I would be more than happy to provide you with a price on the vehicle you mentioned. To best serve you, I would like to e-mail you the price. Please provide me your e-mail address." |
| Customer: | "Just give me your best price over the phone." |
| Sales consultant: | "Mr. Jones, as I am sure you are aware, many dealerships will provide you with a price over the telephone, but then when you arrive at the dealership, the number will have changed. Perhaps the vehicle will no longer be available. Perhaps the sales consultant you spoke with will not be there. For whatever reason, the number will change. Well, we do not play that game. Our company's policy is to provide prices in writing so that we do not end up in a "he said, she said" position. Therefore, if you provide me your e-mail address, I will e-mail you |

| | |
|---|---|
| | our price, which will ensure that there is no misunderstanding." |
| Customer: | "Okay. My e-mail address is..." |
| Sales consultant: | "Thank you. You will receive the e-mail shortly, and I will call you to confirm your receipt of it." |

Then the sales consultant will e-mail the customer the dealership's best price. However, you are going to change the story. Your e-mail will include the following:

- The specifications of the exact vehicle the customer is interested in, including VIN
- The price for the vehicle
- Your bio, which may be in the form of a video (see the chapter on Telephone Techniques)
- A list of all the amenities and extras your dealership provides to customers (e.g., loaner vehicles, refreshments, and pick-up and delivery services)
- Information on certified preowned vehicles with low mileage, ones that are similar to the new vehicle the customer is interested in, including all the specifications, prices, and (if available) videos or photos of the other vehicles

By providing all of this information in your e-mail, you are now competing on the Benefit, not the Cost. Therefore, your price does not have to be as low as those of the other dealerships because you built Value by increasing the benefits and not by reducing the cost. Also, you planted a seed of doubt in the customer's mind about the other dealerships. For example, if the customer goes back to the other dealers and asks if they can provide their prices in writing and if the other dealerships say no, the customer will remember what you said about other dealerships' playing games. Finally, if the customer calls you back and asks if the price you gave was the best one that you could provide, you must say yes, or you would lose all credibility. By the way, if every dealership were to start doing this, then you all would go from competing on prices to competing on benefits—which would produce higher gross profits.

# CHAPTER 18

## FINANCIAL SERVICES

After your customers agree to purchase your vehicles, they will most likely be turned over to an F&I or financial services manager. At some dealerships, sales consultants are executing this step in the process. If sales consultants are facilitating the Financial Services Step at your dealership, then the difference in the execution of this step will revolve around the transition from the sales consultant to the financial services manager since there will not be a transition. Otherwise, the process will be the same.

The execution of this step as an experience rather than as a transaction begins with a warm, personalized introduction that does not increase the customer's anxiety. As a sales consultant, you are transferring the trust the customers have in you to your dealership's financial services manager. If this transfer is done well, customers will have a great experience and will purchase products that will enhance their car-ownership experience. If this transfer is done poorly, you will see the results in your surveys. You always need to be aware that anytime you ask customers to meet with someone else at the dealership, their anxiety will go up. This will especially be the case if it is someone who will be attempting to sell them more products. As a sales consultant, you will need to lower this anxiety, and then your financial services manager will need to continue to lower it before trying to sell anything.

To assist financial services managers in creating experiences for customers, sales consultants should provide customers' personal information to the financial services managers, and the managers can use that information to build rapport. The sales consultants spend much time with the customers during the Sales Process, and the financial services managers only have a short time to build trust and to sell some products and services. If the sales consultants can inform the financial services managers about things the managers may have in common with the customers, the financial services managers can use that information to build rapport and trust in a short period of time. This will be helpful not only in selling additional products and services to the customers but also in creating experiences for them.

Most sales consultants will tell the financial services managers about the length of time the customers are planning to keep their vehicles and whether the customers had extended-service contracts for their previous vehicles. I am asking you to also include personal information, such as favorite sports teams, hobbies, and kids' activities—anything that your financial services manager and customers may have in common.

Your introducing customers to your financial services manager may sound like this: "Mr. Jones, I would like you to meet John. He is our financial services manager. John will complete all of your paperwork and will review with you, among other things, the extended-service contract options, which you and I discussed earlier. One more thing, John is an avid Cubs fan, like you." Prior to the introduction, sales consultants will have already discussed a few topics with the customers.

One of the actions that sales consultants need to perform is to educate customers about the financial services managers and what they will do. Regardless of whether your customers have purchased vehicles before, you want them to know that your dealership is different and that your financial services manager is different too. Sales consultants have to build the benefit of the customers' meeting with the financial services manager. Sales consultants need to use the information gathered from customers to educate them on the importance of what the financial services managers have to offer. This education should happen earlier in the Sales Process.

For example, when a sales consultant is gathering a customer's information that regards the customer's driving habits, the customer (a male) mentions that he likes to keep his vehicles for seven-plus years. Moreover, he says that he usually racks up over seventy-five thousand miles for each vehicle. The sales consultant should then briefly mention that the financial services manager will go over several extended-service contracts that the customer might be interested in because those contracts could protect his investment for the entire time that he owns the car. Before introducing the customer to the manager, the sales consultant should remind the customer about the earlier discussion about the extended-service contracts. In addition, the sales consultant should inform the customer that the manager will review all the paperwork to ensure it is in order and complete. The manager (a female) will discuss financing options that she is qualified to discuss, based on her experience and knowledge, as well as on her knowledge of the customer's financial profile. Finally, the manager will complete all of the motor-vehicle paperwork, thereby eliminating the need for the customer to visit the DMV.

The financial services manager meets the customer at the sales consultant's desk or on the showroom floor. The sales consultant facilitates the introductions and provides the manager with information about the customer's purchase. The manager returns to her office to load the deal information onto her computer, and at that point, the sales consultant walks the customer to the manager's office. While waiting for the manager, the sales consultant needs to be wisely using the customer's time. Depending on how long the wait is, this may include reviewing some of the features of the vehicle or perhaps doing a more formal dealership tour, which could include an introduction to a service consultant or the scheduling of the customer's first service appointment.

After sitting down with the customer, the manager will first review all terms of the sale to confirm that the customer is comfortable with all of the details of the sale. Second, the manager will review other payment options in accordance with the customer's individual needs and wants. Finally, the manager will present products and services to the customer, which will be based on information she or the sales consultant learned from customer. The manager should be using all the skills and techniques that were revealed earlier in this book. Financial services managers are sales people too, so they need to master the skills and techniques used to make sales. For example, financial services managers should use not only listening skills and questioning techniques but also storytelling to increase the benefits of their products.

The Value Equation holds true for the products that are sold by financial services managers. An example of telling a story would be the following passage: "Mr. Jones, you mentioned to Fred, your sales consultant, that you plan to keep your new vehicle for seven years and seventy-five thousand miles. Just last week, a customer visited me. I sold an extended-service contract to this customer six years ago. He was in our service department for a problem with his vehicle. He thanked me for selling him the contract several years ago because without it, his service bill would have been over $2,000." Just like sales consultants, financial services managers need to sell the benefits—not the features—of their products.

Once all the paperwork is complete, the financial services manager will escort the customer back to the sales consultant for the Delivery of the vehicle.

# CHAPTER 19

## DELIVERY

The historical way of delivering vehicles to customers is very transactional. However, the Delivery is a great opportunity to create a memorable experience for customers. The Delivery consists of two parts. The first part is the paperwork; this is the business part and should be treated as such. The customer needs to be reassured that everything is as agreed. The best way to do this is by being transparent and sticking to business. The second part of the Delivery is the actual physical delivery of the vehicle to the customer. This is where customers learn how to use their vehicles, and this second part creates an opportunity for sales consultants or delivery specialists (if your dealership has them) to wow customers by creating a great experience.

First and foremost, the Deliveries of vehicles to customers must be personalized to them. No two deliveries are the same. Sales consultants should tailor the execution of the Deliveries by doing the following:

- Demonstrating vehicle's operating features and paying particular attention to those features that the customer mentioned during the Needs Assessment Step

- Personalizing the setup of the navigation, seats, radio, and so forth, which should be based on the customer's preferences, and educating the customer on how to set these features up by having the customer perform the specific function
- Reviewing the owner's manual with the customer, highlighting and adding bookmarks to those pages that discuss features that the customer mentioned during the Sales Process
- Offering customers an orientation drive
- Having sales managers thank the customers
- Transferring all articles from customers' trade-ins to their new vehicles
- Scheduling customers' first maintenance appointments (if not done earlier)
- Booking a second delivery to review any questions that may arise
- Guiding customers out of delivery bays and thanking them for their purchases

One excellent practice that helps to create a great experience is performing the Deliveries of vehicles with white gloves on and explaining to customers that they should be the first ones who touch the clean vehicles after purchasing them. In addition, all of the radio settings should be preprogrammed to customers' favorite stations, and the navigation systems (if equipped) should be programmed with the customers' home addresses and possibly one or two specific places of interest. Provide customers with small thank-you gifts. These gifts do not have to be extravagant; they could be a key chain, hats, or gift cards to popular coffee shops. Finally, make sure you introduce customers to service advisors, who can discuss with customers all of the great amenities that your service department provides. Also, make sure the advisors schedule customers' first maintenance appointments. If you want your customers to be loyal and keep coming back, make sure they never leave your dealership without appointments to return. Scheduling customers' first service appointments increases the likelihood of their doing business with you in the future.

A great example of how to turn a transaction into an **experience** occurred when I recently had my chimney cleaned. Is there anything more transactional than the cleaning of a chimney? Well, this chimney sweep made it an experience. First, he did an excellent job of cleaning my chimney; he even used drop cloths so that the floor and surrounding area did not get dirty while he worked. After he finished, he suggested that we change the older hoses that connect the water to our washing machine. He said he had seen these hoses break and cause significant water damage. He recommended replacement hoses, which could be purchased at any hardware store for under twenty dollars. Not only did he add value by suggesting something that could potentially save me money and several headaches, but also he "Delivered" my chimney back to me in a way that wowed me. After he was finished, I noticed that there was a lit candle in the fireplace, and it was giving off a wonderful scent. Next to it was a thank-you note. In addition, two days after he was at my home, I received a handwritten thank-you note from him in the mail. It said, "Dear Mr. and Mrs. Wright, It was nice to meet you and a pleasure to serve you. Thank you. Your Chimney Sweep, Fred." This was from a chimney sweep! He took a transaction and made it an experience. You can too.

# CHAPTER 20

## Follow-Up and Creating Customers for Life

You cannot mass-market customer retention. What you do to advertise and market your dealership to get customers to come in cannot be done to retain customers. Sales consultants must develop relationships with their customers to make them want to come back and to prevent them from thinking about going anywhere else. To increase the likelihood of customers' doing business with you in the future, you need to personalize your future contacts.

### Follow-Up

The day after customers take delivery of their vehicles, sales consultants should place calls to the customers, thank them for their business, and ask whether they have any questions about operating their vehicles. Sales consultants can also ask the customers whether they would like to schedule second deliveries to discuss how any of the features work. In addition, sales consultants should mail out handwritten thank-you letters to their customers. The penmanship must be legible, and the notes should do more than just mention a thank-you. These letters should talk about something personal that the sales consultants uncovered about the customers (e.g., children's activities or favorite sports teams). The personal comments can be as simple as "Hope your son's hockey team wins its tournament this weekend." Finally, the thank-you notes can include nominal gift cards to coffee shops or other retail establishments that the customers frequent. Keep two things in mind: your follow-ups must increase the likelihood of your customers' doing business with you again, and the follow-ups cannot be transactional—they must be experiential. Calling your customers to ask them mundane questions—such as how their vehicles are or if they have had a chance to show anyone their new cars or if they can refer someone—is very transactional and will *not* increase the likelihood of your customers' doing business with you in the future. Finally, customers will sometimes write on your survey that they did not receive any follow-up contact—even though you did contact them. In such cases, the reason they do not remember you is because you did not make the follow-ups memorable.

## Creating Customers for Life

To achieve the goals of getting customers to come back to you and to refer their friends to you and your dealership requires that you develop relationships with your customers. Simply contacting customers on predetermined intervals to ask how they are doing or how their vehicles are will not accomplish this. To increase the odds that your customers will keep coming back and refer their friends, you need to contact your customers once per month. I will let that sink in. Yes, I said contact your customers once per month—forever. Breathe and keep reading. Contacting each customer once per month may be hard, but it is not difficult to accomplish. Let me show you how.

First, let me reiterate why it is so important to contact your customers once per month. First, everyone wants referrals. The best referrals are not when your customers tell you about their friends but when they tell their friends about you. The problem is that you never know when their friends will initiate conversations about buying cars. Customers' friends could call the customers the day after you sold them a car or six months later and ask them whom they bought their cars from. The only way your customers will remember you is if you are contacting them once per month. By contacting them once per month, you will remain at the top of their minds. However, this frequent communication only works if your contact is meaningful. Second, the goal is to increase the likelihood of customers' doing business with you in the future. To accomplish this, you must make the monthly contact an experience. By making it an experience, you increase the Benefit of the monthly contact for your customers, and doing so increases Value, which increases the likelihood of customers' doing business with you.

Monthly contact that is meaningful and memorable will create experiences for your customers. However, the contact needs to be more than just telephone calls. Contacting your customers can be done through in-person visits, e-mails, texts, phone calls, letters, or social-networking posts. In the twenty-first century, there are many different media you can use to contact your customers, and within five years, there will probably be more ways to do so. The key is to contact your customers by using their preferred methods of communication. In addition, to truly make your monthly contacts memorable and experiential, they should all be personalized to each customer. The more you know about your customer, the easier this will be.

By the way, even if some customers do not buy vehicles from your dealership, you should still keep in touch with them to ensure that they will buy their next vehicles from you and that they will refer their friends to you. This may not mean contacting them once per month but more likely once per quarter. Even if you cannot personalize the contact, you need to be contacting these customers who did not buy cars from you. They may buy different vehicles from what you sell, but I am sure those vehicles are not the last ones they will buy. You should want to sell them not only their next vehicles but also their next ten. Also, more likely than not (unless of course they read this book), the sales consultants who did sell them cars will not be contacting them after the first follow-ups. Therefore, if you keep in contact with them, not only will you increase the likelihood of selling them their next cars, but also you may get a few referrals from them. Months after customers buy their vehicles, their friends may ask them where they bought their cars, and the customers, since you have been in contact with them, may tell their friends about you rather than the apathetic sales consultants they worked with originally.

I have compiled a list of best practices for contacting customers once per month. As you begin your quest to become the best sales consultant you can be, I am sure you will have more ideas. If possible, all of the contacts need to be personalized. I understand that at first or when contacting an unsold customer, it may not be possible. The personalization can be simple or in depth, depending on the reason for the contact. Once again, these ideas are for sold and unsold customers.

- Respond to customers' online posts, such as the ones on Yelp or DealerRater.
    - Many of your customers may post something on a dealership-rating website. If they do, you should respond to those posts if doing so is appropriate. This means you need to monitor these sites.
- Buy lunch for customers' book-club meetings or card-game days.
    - Customers are just like us: they do such things as play cards and attend book clubs. At most of these get-togethers, food is involved. If you sometimes buy

food for these meetings, your contact with your customers will also serve as a Prospecting activity.

- Send holiday cards to your customers, but also add a QR code that links to a video of you.
    - QR codes were discussed during the chapter on Prospecting. The video can be a simple generic holiday greeting from you (with or without the Santa hat).
- Send Father's Day and Mother's Day cards.
    - Just because they are not your parents doesn't mean you can't send people cards that celebrate the fact that they are parents. In addition, if you are looking for a reason to contact a customer during a month, send a Happy Groundhog Day or Happy Memorial Day e-mail and include something personal (e.g., "Hope your daughter's lacrosse season is going well!").
- E-mail links to articles of interest to your customers, or print the articles and send them to your customers.
    - Once again, the more you know about your customers, the easier this will be. If you read an article that you know they would like, send it to them.
- Do not just go and visit your customers when they bring their vehicles in for service; bring them their favorite drinks or refreshments, and then talk to them about personal things that are happening in their lives.
- Contact your customers for the special events that occur in their lives.
    - Special events are such things as a child being born, a child graduating, a job promotion, and a grandchild being born.
- Contact your customers for their birthdays, anniversaries, and so forth.
    - By anniversaries, I mean their wedding anniversaries, not the anniversaries of when you made money off

> them—that is, when you sold them cars. For most customers, buying cars is not a memorable event. For the few that it is, send them a card.

As I stated, I am confident that you will uncover other ideas as well. Repeat customers are not only the most profitable but also the easiest and best customers to have. First, the relationships you have make the Sales Process enjoyable for you. Second, they are the most profitable customers because they will pay more for your vehicles because of you. By developing relationships with them, you have become a benefit to them. Remember that customers dread going to dealerships. If customers have a trusted advisor at the dealership their visits become much less unpleasant. In this way, YOU have become a Benefit to the customer—so much so that even paying more for your vehicles will not reduce the Value of those vehicles. By executing every step in your Sales Process as an experience, you will increase the likelihood of customers' doing business with you today and in the future.

# CHAPTER 21

## THE CLOSE

This book is the beginning of a process to improve the customer experience in order to sell more vehicles, make more money, and improve customer loyalty. To become an expert at it, you will need to continue learning and practicing your sales craft. At Wright Auto Pro, we provide additional tools and resources that include videos, workbooks, documents to track and measure your success, and training seminars. These resources help bring to life the topics covered in this book. While this book reveals what you should be doing to turn every transaction into an **experience**, the videos on our website will show you how, and our training seminars will provide you with an opportunity to practice these skills and techniques. In addition, if your dealership would like a more personalized training program or in-dealership consulting, we are available for that as well. Our website is www.wrightautopro.com. Finally, the main concept of turning every transaction into an **experience** applies to all customer touch points at every dealership. From sales to service to answering the telephone to greeting a customer on the lot, if you want loyal customers, you need to turn every transaction into an **experience** for your customers. Wright Auto Pro can assist with these other areas as well. My goal is to make all automotive professionals successful.

I have one last point I would like to make. I am a big believer in demographics driving consumption. Based on the changes that have taken place in terms of young people delaying their purchasing of vehicles, it is likely that almost 80 percent of vehicle purchases in the near future will be made by people in the age group 35–74. The US population of this age group from 2000 to 2030 looks like this:

| YEAR | POPULATION (in millions) | Percentage of Population |
|---|---|---|
| 2000 | 125 | 45% |
| 2010 | 144 | 47% |
| 2015 | 158 | 49% |
| 2020 | 159 | 48% |
| 2025 | 165 | 48% |
| 2030 | 170 | 47% |

Taking this table of information into account and given that new vehicle sales in the United States in 2000 was 17.3 million and in 2015 was 17.4 million, it would seem logical that the new vehicle sales number will stay the same or will increase over the next few years. The question you will have to ask yourself is, "Will I get my share of these sales?" If you turn every transaction into an **experience** by executing your Sales Process in accordance with this book's guidelines, the answer will be an unequivocal YES!

## ABOUT THE AUTHOR

The automobile industry has been a big part of Douglas Wright's life. He grew up around his father's Mercedes-Benz dealership.

Wright attended Syracuse University, after which he worked as a Wall Street portfolio manager for two years. He then returned to college to obtain his MBA from Columbia University.

In 1996, Wright purchased a Chrysler, Dodge, and Jeep dealership in Upstate New York. Over the next decade, he purchased four underperforming dealerships, revitalized them, and sold them for a profit.

Wright left the retail side of the auto industry in 2002 to found Wright Auto Pro. Wright Auto Pro develops and delivers performance-improvement solutions to increase dealership sales and profits. To date, Wright has provided performance solutions to over five hundred dealerships in North America.

Wright has created dozens of training classes and regularly publishes in Dealer magazine. More information about Wright Auto Pro can be found at www.wrightautopro.com.

## WORKS CITED


Karesky, Tess. "Women Buy Cars Too." CDK Global Special Report 2015

Burke, Kathleen. "Millennials top Gen X in new-car buying for first time." *Automotive News,* August 1, 2014.

Debord, Matthew. "Actually, we were all wrong – millennials love cars." *Business Insider,* November 14, 2016.

Durbin, Dee-Ann. "4 reasons millennials are buying cars in big numbers." *Chicago Tribune,* March 20, 2016.

Bond, Vince. "Report: Low desire for online buying." *Automotive News,* October 10, 2016.

Kurz, Christopher, Geng Li, and Daniel Vine. "The Young and the Carless? The Demographics of New Vehicle Purchases." *FEDS Notes,* June 24, 2016.

Rowe, Jared. "New Autotrader Study: Consumers Want Big Changes to the Car Buying Process." *Autotrader,* March 31, 2015.

Verdon, Joan. "Niches stock the shelves." *The Record,* November 4, 2016.

LeBeau, Phil. "Americans rethinking how they buy cars." *CNBC.com,* February 26, 2014.

Rockwood, Kate. "Need to boost your sales? This surprising new research will help." *Inc Magazine,* March 2017.

Lynn, Kathleen. "Putting in a good word for homes." *The Record,* March 17, 2017.

Bazilian, Emma. "Infographic: How storytelling is helping brands sell more products." *ADWEEK,* January 16, 2017.

De Groote, Michael. "Study proves people hate to shop for cars." *Taunton Daily Gazette,* April 30, 2014.

Hamilton, Jared. "2015 DrivingSales Consumer Experience Research Study." *DrivingSales.com*

27862189R00083

Made in the USA
Columbia, SC
08 October 2018